The
Science
Of
SELLING

By Dr. D. Paul Reilly

The Reilly Institute
P.O.Box 7121
Nassau Bahamas

The Reilly Institute
P.O.Box 7121
Nassau Bahamas
Tel 242-422-4455
www.DPaulReilly.com

DEDICATION

This book is dedicated to the greatest salesman I ever knew, Thomas Anthony Reilly, my father, who departed this life on May 30th, 1976.

Contents

FOREWORD 7

PREFACE 9

INTRODUCTION 11

PREPARATION 13

PERSONAL APPEARANCE... 23

ENTHUSIASM.. 27

PLANNING 31

PERSISTENCY 35

HOW TO ACT 41

SETTING SALES GOALS 45

ADVERTISING AND PUBLIC RELATIONS...................... 51

REFERRALS... 57

OVER-SELLING 63

RECORD KEEPING 67

SERVICE AFTER SALES 71

FURTHER EDUCATION 75

COMMUNICATION 79

HONESTY.. 89

BE INNOVATIVE AND CREATIVE 93

ALWAYS A PROFESSIONAL 97

PATIENCE AND TACT 103

SHOWMANSHIP.. 109

SELF-CONCEPT/SELF-ESTEEM 113

PROBLEM SOLVING 119

SELF-DISCIPLINE... 125

SOME VERY VITAL ATTRIBUTES 129

HEALTH OF MIND AND BODY.. 135

SELLING BY ASKING QUESTIONS 139

ACTION 143

CLOSING... 147

FOREWORD

I like a book in which the author has something worthwhile to say. And who says it clearly, succinctly and persuasively. A writer who outlines in his table of contents what his book is all about, and who then proceeds to develop his material in a logical, clear-cut, and interesting manner is sure to keep me going as one of his readers.

Such a writer is D. Paul Reilly, whose second book, THE SCIENCE OF SELLING, I have just had opportunity to read in manuscript form. Because I found real values in his first book, SUCCESS IS SIMPLE, I approached this second book with anticipation. And I was not disappointed, for here we have a work on selling that is one of the most down-to-earth, sensible, and practical dissertations on the subject of selling that I have read in recent years. Any salesman who wants to improve himself and his performance will find sound guidance in this book, THE SCIENCE OF SELLING.

For many years I have been speaking to large audiences of salespeople all over North America. I like salesmen and saleswomen, for usually they are outgoing, positive-thinking, and therefore inspiring people. I think that I know something of their needs and their problems and can assure them that they will find in Mr. Reilly's new book answers that really answer. It is filled with creative suggestions which, if acted upon, are bound to make better people, and naturally better people make better salesmen. hat a salesman is has plenty to do with what a salesman sells. The book is a veritable how-to-do-it document, and if its wise and tested procedures are followed by the reader it is hard to see how he or she can help turning in a better sales record.

I am impressed by Mr. Reilly's explicitness, a quality that no doubt grows not only out of his nature, but also out of his long personal experience in selling. It is a profession in which he has been outstandingly successful. In his book he makes crystal clear the success secrets he has found in his own career. He is therefore a good teacher, as well as writer.

I warmly commend his book to all who truly desire self-improvement.

Norman Vincent Peale

PREFACE

I have for many years and particularly since the publication of my first book "Success is Simple," desired to write a book on professional selling. Now at last at 4:00 a.m. on this beautiful Monday morning, August 23rd, 1976, I am finally taking the necessary **action** and putting my thoughts on paper.

There have been many books written on the subject of selling. Many of them by people who have never. ever sold a product or service, in other words it is al I theory and as we all know theory and practice are indeed two entirely different things. I therefore feel amply justified in writing this book having been actually engaged in direct selling and I do not mean "order-taking," there is of course a vast difference! For over 30 years in all parts of the world, Europe, Canada, North and South America, The Bahamas, Bermuda and the Caribbean. I have personally sold a great deal of products and services both tangible and intangible and I am proud to say that whatever I sold, and wherever I sold once even through an interpreter in

Vienna, Austria and for whichever organization I sold I was continuously the best the top of the list salesperson with that particular organization. I am therefore qualified to write this book on the greatest of all professions "Selling!" This book will be a practical one rather than a theoretical one and it is written in the spirit that it will help many a sales person, young or old, new to the profession or experienced or even the sales manager or sales director to do a better job of selling professionally, to making a great contribution to their nation's overall economy. Always remember that no matter what product or service a country has such as tourism it must be sold… nothing happens until someone sells something! One final note to each and every salesperson around the world I feel that you should be very proud of your chosen profession and. fully understand and realize that you, play a very important part in the overall economy of your particular country and the entire world. I believe it is really exciting to be able to make such a tremendous contribution to society .... to be a salesperson!

August 23rd, 1976

D. Paul Reilly
Nassau, Bahamas

INTRODUCTION

"No other trade or profession has more opportunity to rise from poverty to great wealth than that of salesman."

O.G. Mandino

Those of you who have already read my first book "Success Is Simple" will be familiar with the fact that I like to be extremely explicit in what I am saying and give many dictionary definitions throughout my writings. The reasons for this method of mine is that (A) I am a very explicit, precise and specific person and (B) I know, and I am sure many of you do that too many people in this world today do not understand what they are either saying or writing about! So at least let us all understand what is written on the pages of this book — thus my dictionary definitions.

The American College Dictionary defines **To Sell** as "To give up or make over to another for a consideration." Webster's Dictionary says that to sell is "To dispose of for an equivalent usually money." A great sales trainer that I once heard, said selling is (A) finding out what the prospect needs and wants and filling those needs and (B) it is teaching. Webster's Dictionary defines **Science** in part as (A) "Truth ascertained by observation, experiment, and induction" and (B) "Ordered arrangements of facts known under classes or heads, knowledge of principles and rules."

I have therefore set out in the pages of this book the basic laws and truths of professional selling which I have ascertained by observation, experiment and induction and which are presented here as an ordered arrangement of facts known under classes or heads together with my knowledge of principals and rules of professionalism. If these laws and principles are put into practice as suggested, they will assist you in learning to sell if you are new to the profession or to improve your selling techniques (if you have been selling for a number of years) or to teach others to sell (if you are involved in sales management or training). So on with the show! .... Good reading! .... and good selling!!

1

PREPARATION

"Failure will never overtake me if my determination to succeed is strong enough."

O.G. Mandino

No pilot would get into an aircraft and attempt to fly it from New York to London without first obtaining the necessary training and practical knowledge to fly that aircraft across the Atlantic otherwise there would be a disaster. Well selling is no different from any other profession in that you must prepare yourself for the task at hand and prepare yourself well, for the better your preparation, the better the end results, the more sales.

Now what are the basics that you must learn before commencing actual sales calls? (Preferably with a sales manager or supervisor). They are: — (A) Full product or service knowledge (B) The ability to prospect (C) The learning by heart of a prepared "sales presentation" (D) Learning how to break the preoccupation barrier and (E) developing positive mental attitude. Now there is much more knowledge and many more principles and skills which you will learn throughout the chapters of this book to help make you a polished professional salesperson. But I am suggesting that before you even make your first sales call you master the above five principles in detail.

PRODUCT OR SERVICE KNOWLEDGE

So let us start with (A) **Full product or service knowledge**. You must understand that although the basic principles of selling are the same no matter what product or service you are selling. You must first obtain a thorough knowledge of the particular product or service that you are about to sell. To more fully illustrate this particular fact let us once again talk about the trained pilot who can fly (let us say a D.C. 9 Aircraft) all over the United States without any problems. He is fully familiar with every aspect, every instrument and literally knows this particular aircraft backwards. He is a good pilot and can fly the D.C. 9 anywhere in good or even bad weather and under a variety of different conditions which may occur. Now he gets a promotion and has to fly the new wide-bodied jet the D.C. 10. on Trans-Atlantic flights. We already know that he is an excellent pilot with many many miles of flying in the D.C. 9 behind him and yet before he is even allowed to attempt to take control of the D.C. 10, he has to first go through a series of simulator tests. (A simulator for those of you who are not familiar with it is a mock up cabin of a D.C. 10 which gives the actual effects of real flight although it never leaves the ground.) The pilot must get used to the new instrument panel, the new take-off and landing speeds, etc. Then he will be checked out in an actual D.C. 10 aircraft for several flying hours before he is certified or qualified to actually fly it and carry passengers in it. Well as I said at the beginning although the actual principles of selling are the same no matter what the product or service is you as a professional salesperson must be checked out and have gained a complete knowledge of the particular product or service which you are about to sell (be it automobiles, real estate, advertising or insurance).

The first thing that any reputable company does when they take on staff to train as salespeople is to fully acquaint them with their products and services, usually by a series of training seminars. Then attending such seminars be very attentive, take notes, and pay full attention as this is really going to help you sell the particular product or service. It is important then to con-tinue to keep on learning by getting books and trade magazines and attending any further courses that you can to become a truly professional sales person. Remember that just because you are an excellent automobile salesperson it does not automatically follow that you will be a great real estate salesperson until you have fully learned and understood your new product or service. So please do concentrate on the product or service that you are selling and gain the fullest knowledge of it as it will in the end determine your dollar volume in sales. People in this day and age are not stupid or over-trusting, so they are going to ask a lot of questions about your product or service and if you wish to **sell** then you better have **all** of the answers, otherwise in most cases you will lose the sale!

Product or service knowledge is therefore vital to being a professional salesperson.

And now let us move on to (B) as mentioned at the beginning of this chapter.

PROSPECTING

THE ABILITY TO PROSPECT

Firstly you must learn and fully understand the difference between a "suspect" and a "prospect." A suspect is just the name of any person you may know. Whereas a prospect is a **qualified** suspect. In other words, if you are an automobile salesperson and wish to sell a person a Lincoln Continental, you will be completely wasting your time even attempting to sell this high-priced automobile to a person whose income will not make it possible to keep up the payments or make the down payment. So you must do some serious research when compiling your prospect list. Who is the person? What are their preferences? What is their income? What can they afford? Armed with this information you are then equipped to come up with a product or service that will immediately appeal to your **qualified** prospect. So when dealing with prospects you must first do your homework and learn as much as possible about them for otherwise you are literally wasting your time as in all probability you will be trying to sell them a product or service which they either do not want or cannot afford.

Now let us move on to (C).

THE LEARNING BY HEART OF A "PREPARED SALES PRESENTATION"

Many salespersons with a natural flair for selling (you might say the born salesperson) do not fully understand the importance of earning by heart word for word a **"Prepared Sales Presentation"** and then having the ability to deliver that **"Sales Presentation"** just like an actor, again and again, literally thousands of times, each time as if it were the very first time that you ever said those words.

Remember and never forget that a salesperson is an actor, a fair salesperson is a fair actor, an excellent professional salesperson is just the same as an excel lent professional actor. Every word, every sentence is articulated and delivered with true conviction. So before you ever make a sales call learn by heart your **"Prepared Sales Presentation,"** and if by chance you are interrupted in the middle of it by a series of questions do not let it upset you but instead having politely answered the queries get right back into the **"Prepared Sales Presentation"** and start off from where you were interrupted.

Is a prepared sales presentation important for the professional salesperson? You better believe it is . . . without it you are finished before you start!

BREAKING THE PREOCCUPATION BARRIER

Now to point (D) raised at the beginning of this chapter on preparation learning **"How to break the preoccupation barrier."** It is import ant for you to understand that your call is an interruption on your prospect. You have to get the prospect to stop thinking about what he was thinking about before you arrived and get and keep his undivided attention to you and your product or service. Here are several suggestions for "breaking the preoccupational barrier" (1) Use a sample or a gift. (2) Use a referral (there will be more about this in Chapter 9). (3) Pay a sincere compliment. (4) Arouse curiosity. (5) Show or exhibit a brochure, video film etc. (6) Deliver a startling statement. (7) Render a service, for example a monthly newsletter. (8) Ask a question as the prospect must think to answer your question. These questions should be open-ended questions, starting with any of the following words, who, why, which, what, where, how? An answer must be given; thus, you will break the preoccupational barrier and will go on to sell (A) yourself and (B) your product or service.

POSITIVE MENTAL ATTITUDE

And now to the final point raised at the beginning of this chapter (E) **Developing a positive mental attitude.** You know every sale is either made or not made by the salesperson in their own mind before they ever meet the prospect. I know that this always has worked for me and can for you too, but it takes constant practice. You must have a positive mental attitude and truly believe in your heart and soul that there is no way possible for you not to sell your product or service.

Now let me give you a specific example from my own selling career which will perhaps illustrate better how I (A) obtained a thorough knowledge of my product (B) prospected effectively (C) learned my prepared "sales presentation" (D) Continually broke the preoccupation barrier and (E) maintained a positive or winning mental attitude.

I had learnt about the Earl Nightingale Motivational and Sales Training Audio Cassette Programmes and decided to go to their home office in Chicago to inquire about taking out a dealership for the Bahamas. I flew to Chicago from Nassau on a Sunday evening. I spent most of Sunday night and early Monday morning listening to the Nightingale tapes. Monday, I went to the home office, singed a dealership agreement, got some instruction on selling the programmes from my good friend Ron Davis, headed for O'Hare Airport and flew back to Nassau via Miami. When I returned to Nassau I proceeded to spend two days listening to all of the cassettes in all of the programmes and making notes, I then commenced calling all of the large insurance companies in Nassau and setting up appointments. Next I learnt by heart the "prepared sales presentation" which the Nightingale-Conant Corporation had given me. When actually making my calls, I opened with "I represent Earl Nightingale," the world's most listened to radio personality, (this really did break the preoccupation barrier) and perhaps most important of all I knew in my mind that I would be successful in selling large quantities of these programmes. I had a positive mental attitude. The end result was that in just five weeks I sold 27,000.00 worth of these Motivational and Sales Training Audio — Cassette Programmes which was a world record among the 4,000 Earl Nightingale communications distributors. So my "preparation" paid off very well indeed.

You will find that once you have mastered these five main principles you are at least ready to hit the road and start with an experienced salesperson, supervisor or sales manager in order that he can assist you when you make mistakes and can also motivate you when you do not make every sale. So out you go now and start on the road to the top in the greatest profession in the world "Salesmanship!"

2

PERSONAL APPEARANCE

"Unless a man looks the part, people won't believe what he says is important."

Frank Bettger

"He has, I know not what of greatness in his looks, and of high fate that he almost awes me."

Dryden

I am quite sure that all of us realize that first impressions are very important indeed. This is particularly important for the salesperson. We mentioned in Chapter One the importance of breaking the pre-occupation barrier. ell by being well dressed, well groomed, having a good-looking car. and a generally pleasing personality you will be helping to break this preoccupation barrier and also helping to create confidence with your prospect. This is particularly important if this is your first call on a prospect. Every single part of your overall appearance is indeed important, your personal hygiene, the neatness of the grooming of your hair, your shirt (always clean and well pressed), your tie (impressive but rather conservative), your suit (again well-pressed and businesslike), your shoes always shining, your fingernails well-manicured, your breath fresh (there are many brand name, very inexpensive makes of breath fresheners) and of course it goes without saying an overall cleanly odour. Use plenty of quality aftershave, deodorant and if a lady, a quality not too strong perfume. Remember that you sell yourself first and then the product or service and in selling yourself personal appearance and good grooming is absolutely essential.

The above details may sound a little overdone but if you wish to prove the point why not try the opposite to what I have recommended above and then do as I have recommended, and you will immediately notice the difference in the volume of your sales and how much easier it is to get the actual interview. Remember I speak from over thirty years of practical experience in the field of selling and direct marketing and although this chapter may appear to be rather short believe you me its contents are extremely important.

Again let me inject a personal example from my own selling career. When I resigned from the Nightingale-Conant Corporation as Regional Director for the Bahamas, Bermuda, the Caribbean, Central and South America to go into business for myself, I commenced correspondence and telephone conversations with a small organization called "Goals Inc." of Amarillo, Texas, U.S.A. This company had some excellent audio cassette personal development programmes but not too much marketing know-how or financial backing at that time. Now I went to Amarillo and spent three days with J.C. Christopher, the chairman of the organization. I came away from Amarillo with an exclusive 10-year agreement to sell all of the products of "Goal Inc." in every English-speaking country throughout the world (except the United States).

This was a fantastic agreement and thus was born "Goals International Limited." I became that company's chairman and chief executive officer with offices in Amarillo, Texas, Nassau, Bahamas, Miami, Florida and London, England. I truly believe that apart from my negotiating and selling ability my overall **personal appearance** helped greatly in assisting me to finalize the agreement. I really **looked** the part.

So continually look your very best for this will also make you feel good inside, give you greater all-round confidence and increase your self-esteem and sales volume. Personal appearance is indeed important for the professional salesperson.

3

ENTHUSIASM

"Nothing is so contagious as enthusiasm; it is the real allegory of the Tale of Orpheus; it moves stones. It charms brutes. Enthusiasm is the genius of sincerity and truth accomplishes no victories without it."

Bulwer

"No enthusiast ever yet could rest 'til half mankind were like himself possess'd"

Cowper

Webster's Dictionary defines enthusiasm as "Passionate zeal for a person, object or pursuit. Keen interest," and an enthusiast as "one who is carried away by enthusiasm." The American College Dictionary describes enthusiasm as "absorbing or controlling possession of the mind by any interest or pursuit; lively interest" and an enthusiast as "one who is filled with enthusiasm for some principle pursuit etc., a person of ardent zeal." The same dictionary describes zeal as "Ardour for a person, cause, or object; eager desire or endeavour, enthusiastic diligence."

So you can see from the above quotes and dictionary definitions that enthusiasm is vital for the salesperson who really wishes to succeed in their chosen profession and reach the top of the ladder. Enthusiasm is not automatic but once it is practiced with one's fellow salespeople or prospects it is infectious and eventually everyone will be enthusiastic about you, and your product or service and will be buying it. What I mean when I say that "enthusiasm" is not automatic is this . . . . . we do not feel fantastic everyday of our lives no matter how good our product or service is and how much we believe in it. Let's face it everyone has bad days — I know I certainly do. But it is like everything else in life, if you want to be successful, you must work on it and practice it. When I feel down some days, I use this self-motivating phrase given to me by W. Clement Stone "I feel happy! I feel healthy! I feel terrific!" If you repeat this phrase several times out loud with true feelings of conviction, you will soon feel enthusiastic and as I said, before your prospects will notice it and they too will become enthusiastic about you and your product or service and will ultimately buy. It is not easy but like everything else in life if you wish to succeed you must stay with it and constantly work on it.

You should make a practice of daily and before each call mentally preparing yourself and using that self-motivator "I feel happy! I feel healthy! I feel terrific!" It really works. So why not try it and start working on your enthusiasm for it **will** work wonders for you, open up previously closed doors and result in greatly increased sales, to say nothing of that wonderful inner peace of mind and satisfaction that accompanies helping to make others feel enthusiastic. Enthusiasm is very contagious as illustrated by this story.

A man climbed into a barber's chair and asked "where is the barber who used to work on the next chair?" "Oh that was a sad case" the barber said, "he became so nervous and despondent over poor business, that one day when a customer said he did not want a massage, he went out of his mind and cut the customer's throat with a razor. He is now in the state mental hospital. By the way" said the barber **enthusiastically** to his customer "would you like a massage, sir?" Extremely enthusiastically replied the customer "Absolutely! Absolutely!"

A good example which comes to mind of how being really enthusiastic paid off for me in a fantastic sales bonus, happened in 1968 on the Island of Grand Cayman (population 8,500 people) in the Cayman Islands. At that time I represented an English organization called "International Learning Systems" and was selling an educational package which included the world famous "Chambers Encyclopedia." I remember it well, it was a beautiful Sunday (one of the best days for selling books as both parents are usually home). I left my hotel bubbling over with enthusiasm at about 12 noon and returned to the hotel at 7:30 p.m. in time for a well-earned dinner. How well did my enthusiasm pay off? Well believe it or not in that 7 ½ hour period on this small sparsely-populated sunny Caribbean Island, I set another world record for "International Learning Systems" by selling 12 sets of encyclopedias at $402.00 per set or a total of $4,824.00 for my afternoon's work. I was getting at that time $45.00 per sale commission and therefore I personally made $540.00 for my Sunday afternoon's work. Enthusiasm made the difference!

So do work on your enthusiasm. As it is another great attribute which will assist you in becoming a great professional salesperson. Remember an old proverb says "A man without a smile should never open a shop." Enthusiasm does make the difference between the fair and the great salesperson ...... take your choice.

4

PLANNING

"Then schemes are laid in advance, it is surprising how often the circumstances fit in with them."

Sir William Osler

"It is surprising how much I can get done when I take enough time for planning and it is perfectly amazing how little I get done without it."

Frank Bettger

Planning is without any doubt one of the most important ingredients, laws, principles or rules, which go into any successful career and this is particularly true for the career minded professional salesperson. Time to the salesperson is literally, money and time wasted by inadequate planning will result in a considerable loss in money and sales. The successful professional salesperson must have a design to attain his sales goals (which we will discuss in greater detail in Chapter 7). He must be organized, the exact order for his day must be explicitly set out. He must have designed a definite programme by careful forward short and long-range planning to achieve his predetermined sales goals. His strategy must be mapped out. He must shape out a course, prepare, systemize and organize his work most diligently, otherwise he will definitely not achieve his goals.

Webster's Dictionary describes a plan in part as "to arrange beforehand" and the American College Dictionary states that a plan, project, design, scheme implies "a formulated method of doing something" and continues "plan refers to any method of thinking out our acts and purposes beforehand." Having given you these specific definitions let me openly ask you "What are your plans for today? This week? This month? Next month? For this year? For the next 5/10 years? For your life? If you wish to become a top professional salesperson you should set aside time daily or at least weekly for the planning of all of your activities, prospecting, making calls, furthering your education of your particular product or service and of increasing your sales volume and income. So once again take it from a 30-year veteran professional salesman that if you wish to become successful in this great profession you must start and continue daily to plan your total activities as a salesperson. If you do not know where you are going, how can you ever hope to arrive.

I always plan all of my activities well in advance. I, at this point, in time have three more books planned over the next two years. A specific example of how careful and detailed long-range planning helped me to sell some $100,000.00 worth of product occurred in 1970. I had a particular sales training audio cassette programme which was specifically designed for Life Underwriters. So I decided to concentrate on selling this particular product throughout the entire Caribbean area. Firstly, I wrote away to the telephone companies in every country in the region and requested a telephone directory. Upon receiving the telephone directories, I looked in the yellow pages and got the names and addresses of all the leading life insurance companies. I then took my diary and set out a very specific six-month plan of travel which would take me to every major country in the area. Having finalized my travel plans, I wrote to the manager of every company enclosing a brochure of the programme I was selling and stated that I would call on them at a particular time and date. I then took the necessary action and proceeded to put my plans in motion. Over a six-month period, I traveled all over the Caribbean, Central and South America. Traveling thousands of miles and making hundreds of calls in Jamaica, Puerto Rico, the U.S., Virgin Islands, Antigua, Dominica, Barbados, Trinidad, Guyana and Belize. By the end of this six-month carefully planned sales drive, I had sold over $100,000.00 worth of product. The campaign was highly successful, but I could not have even broken the ice if I had not made very careful, definite and specific long-range plans. So fellow salespeople please for your sake remember this most important principle of selling and marketing. Set aside time to plan your sales activities as planning and organization is a time saver and time to you means money, a greater number of calls and ultimately a higher volume of sales. Planning is therefore vitally important!

This story on planning I thought was amusing. The social worker was trying to help in a rehabilitation programme at the prison "Do you have any plans for the future when you are released?" He asked the prisoner. "Yes" replied the prisoner "I've got the plans of two jewelry stores and a bank to start with!" So much for planning and now on to our next Chapter 5 entitled "Persistency."

5

PERSISTENCY

"Success comes to those who try - and keep on trying"

W. Clement Stone

"I will persist until I succeed."

O.G. Mandino

Here is a story which amuses me and at the same time fully illustrates what persistency is which I hope you will enjoy too.

The tramp went to the back door of a pub/restaurant in Devon, England with the fairly common name there of "George And The Dragon." "I haven't had anything to eat for days" he said to the rather unpleasant-looking woman who appeared to be in charge. "Do you think you could spare me something to eat?" "Certainly not" she shouted, "We don't feed tramps here!" "Thank you" said the tramp and went away. However, he was **persistent** and a few minutes later he was back. "What do you want now?" the same lady asked, even more annoyed than ever. "Could I have a few words with George?" asked the tramp. But seriously after thirty years of professional salesmanship I personally feel that persistency is perhaps one of **the** most important rules for success in professional selling. I also feel that it is one of the most difficult parts of selling or marketing for you must be prepared to take nine straight "**no's**" in a row to your well-rehearsed sales presentation (which I referred to under the heading Item C in Chapter 1) given with great enthusiasm (Chapter 3) and acted out word for word like the master actor the true professional salesman that you are and still go on to the tenth prospect and again with all the enthusiasm you can muster up and with a smile in your heart and on your face give that presentation again and come out triumphant with the sale. Persistency is quite definitely vital to the successful professional salesperson. Even if you do not sell every prospect (and you will not) take his name down and transfer it to one of your prospect cards (we will deal with this in more detail in Chapter 11 "Record Keeping") and in another three months call again on this same prospect perhaps with a slightly different approach or a different product or service that your company has to offer.

I can assure you that I personally haoove again and again made substantial sales to prospects who have previously said no. Simply by using a different approach or offering a new product of service. Some prospects will get annoyed with you (but that is all a part of selling too!) But you will be amazed at how many will respect you for your courage, determination, guts and persistency and will buy your product and become a permanent customer or client. So do be persistent and never give up after all if you fully believe in your product or service (and if you do not you should not be selling it at all) you are really doing your prospect a favour in being persistent and helping him to make the right decision to purchase your product or service. Keep this in mind as it will greatly assist you in being consistently persistent. Finally to more fully illustrate this point of persistency I would like to tell you the story of a man who lived in the 1800's in the United States of America. He had a very difficult childhood, had less than one year's formal schooling, failed in business twice in 1831 and 1833, he went into politics and lost a total of nine elections in 1832, 1838, 1840, 1843, 1848, 1855, 1856 (for vice-president) and again in 1858 for the senate. In 1835, his fiancée (whom he loved dearly) died. He did marry in 1842 but only one of four sons lived past the age of 18. This is true story of a man who even though his failures were many and his successes were few was persistent and never gave up for in 1860 he became President of the United States of America and was one of the most beloved and respected presidents in that nation's history. His name.... Abraham Lincoln.

It is indeed easy for me to recall an occasion when persistency really paid off for me as a salesperson. For it was at the very start of my career in my native Dublin, Ireland, I was just 17 at the time and home from college for the summer vacation. My father and mother ran a factory called "Taraware Limited " and manufactured a large variety of religious medals and jewelry. I got a job with them for the summer and set out with great determination and enthusiasm to become a great salesperson. I called first on one of "Taraware's biggest accounts (you see I always thought big even at age 17). The name of the company was "Aranha Bros." The managing director, Mr. Bert Aranha who did all of the buying was not in. To cut a long story short, I spent some five weeks and more than 15 actual calls before I eventually met with Mr. Arahna. **However persistency** did pay off for I got the largest order that "Taraware Ltd." had ever got from this company. Many years later my father told me that he had met with Bert Aranha, and he had said that he gave the big order because he appreciated my **persistency**. To use his own words, he said that "I was a go-getter!" So persistency is indeed important to the professional salesperson. And now let us finish this chapter with the immortal words of one of the world's great statesmen Winston Churchill who said "This is the lesson: Never give in... never... never... never... in nothing, great or small, large or petty — never give in except to convictions of honour or good taste." So much for persistency and now on to Chapter Six entitled "How to Really Act."

6

HOW TO ACT

"An actor is a sculptor who carves in snow."

Lawrence Barrett

"To see him act, is like reading Shakespeare by flashes of lightning (of Edmund Kean)."

S. T. Coleridge

"All the world's a stage."

Shakespeare

Although this book is obviously intended to be a serious textbook for the professional salesperson, I feel that a well-placed joke or two makes it easier to read and enjoy. I really do want you to learn from this book and also to enjoy it… thus now and then I throw in a story when it fits in with the actual subject material that I am writing about. This story about an actor really amused me and I hope it tickles your fancy too!

A budding young actor came home enthused about an assignment in a new play. "Dad, guess what?" he said. "I got my first part. I play the part of a man who has been married for 25 years." "That's a good start son" said his father. "Just keep at it and one of these days you'll get a speaking part." Now joking apart your ability to act, to deliver the same lines (your "prepared sales presentation") dozens, maybe hundreds of times a day and each time make it sound as if it was the first time that you had ever said it to a prospect is going to (without a shadow of a doubt) determine how good a professional salesperson you will be!!

You should consider your sales presentation and the time you spend with your prospect delivering it as a play and you're the lead actor in this play. You must perform like a master actor delivering each and every sentence with conviction. Vary the tone of your voice by putting eat emphasis on the advantages of your product or service! Smile, look sad even shock at times. Use your hands, move about, change the expressions on your face. Act! Act! Act! And if you act your part with excellence ·the close will be automatic and the sale yours as the curtain finally drops on a good performance.

Do not forget all actors have to first learn their lines and then rehearse them until they are ready for opening night to go on stage. Well as a professional salesperson you must do the same as suggested in Chapter 1 (preparation). You must learn your sales presentation off by heart. I find that a good way to do this is by using a cassette tape recorder. Record the entire presentation acting it out as if you were really with a prospect and then sit back and listen to yourself over and over again. The learning process is listening to things repeatedly, so the tape recorder will help you out considerably in this area. Then you should start to really rehearse the presentation with another person. At many company sales training courses, they have role playing sessions where one person is the prospect and another prospect and another prospect and another out the actual sale. You can also rehearse at home with your husband or wife, mother or father, brother or sister.

Finally, you can act the whole presentation out by yourself in front of a mirror. Only when you feel that you are ready and fully rehearsed should you go in to make your presentation.

As acting is indeed an integral part of selling it is difficult for me to pick out a particular incident in my sales career which may help to fully illustrate the importance of good acting in good selling. However, early in my career I was working in England for a London-based company "Ensley Displays Limited." This company was in the theatre publicity business and my job was visiting all types of businesses and selling them the idea of having an illuminated display stand in their window advertising the local theatre and also displaying their goods. There was a set "sales presentation " which I (even to this day) know of by heart and I believe I could say it in my sleep. It was only a short ten-minute sales presentation but extremely effective. Now I delivered this "sales presentation" on an average of 50 times a day, five days a week for over four years all over the British Isles in England, Ireland, Scotland and Wales. I therefore delivered this same "sales presentation" over 50,000 times but it consistently obtained the desired results for I was continuously the top salesperson and eventually sales manager for "Ensley Displays Limited" until my resignation to go into business for myself. I believe that every time I delivered my "sales presentation" to my prospects it sounded as though it was the **first** time I had ever said it. Acting made the difference.

One final suggestion is to join a local amateur drama club I am sure there are several in your area. It is a wonderful hobby and it will also be assisting you greatly in your chosen profession as a master salesperson.

7

SETTING SALES GOALS

"What the mind can conceive and believe, it can achieve."

Dr. Napoleon Hill

"The trouble with men is not in achieving their goals, it is in setting them."

Earl Nightingale

Anyone's personal success depends to a great deal on their ability to set predetermined goals (both immediate, intermediate, ultimate, short and long range) and to achieve those goals on target this applies in a person's business and personal life.

In the selling profession the setting of specific sales goals and achieving them on target is absolutely essential. So now let us define accurately exactly what a goal is, how to set goals and exactly what a goal is, how to set goals and Firstly the American College Dictionary defines a goal as "that toward which effort is directed" and Webster's Dictionary states that a goal is "an object or effort, an end or aim." so we can plainly see that unless we have a series of specific sales goals predetermined at the beginning of each year, we are not going to sell large quantities of our products or services or become super sales people. So to state it simply, a sales goal is that dollar volume of sales that a person has set for themselves for a given specific period in advance. Now how do you go about setting sales goals or setting your sales projections for a day, a week, a month and for the whole year.

Well with most big companies particularly in the insurance industry they help you to set your sales goals for each year. To the novice working for a small company or even for themselves. Let me recommend this method. Sit down at the beginning of the year with a blank sheet of paper and list out your total expenses for the year. The house mortgage payment, the car finance payment, the children's education fees, office rent (if you are in business for yourself), funds for a vacation. Clothes, insurance, medical expenses and literally every expense which you know you are going to have to meet (including income or sales taxes where these apply). When you total up all of these figures I suggest you add on 10% of this total figure for unseen expenses, and contingencies. Add another 10% to go into your savings account and then add at least 35% more as your profit for your year's work.

Example: Total Annual Expenses	$10,000.00
10% Contingencies	1,000.00
10% Savings Account	1,000.00
35% Profit	3,500.00

Total	$15,500.00

So now you know that you have to earn $15,500.00 during the coming year. Divide that figure by 2, which will tell you that you must earn $1,291.00 per month, divide this by four and you know that you must earn $322.00 per week. Divide this figure by five and you get a daily figure of $64.00 which you **must** earn to achieve the annual dollar sales goal which you have set for yourself. Now depending on whether you are paid by salary plus commission or only by commission and depending on the product or service and average cost of your product or service you will then know exactly how much of your product you should sell each day to earn that $64.00. You will also know exactly how many calls you are going to **have** to make in order to achieve your daily quota or sales goal.

Now here is how you can achieve these goals on target. The only way to make **sales** is by making **calls** and if you keep on making the **calls** you must make the sales. It is just the law of averages. When you have set your sales goals, write them down and make sure that you check each day to make sure you are on target. If for some reason you have had a bad week this week and have not reached your predetermined sales goals you will just have to pull out all the stops next week to make up for it. I feel that a person should increase their earnings by at least 10% each year. So next year's goal should be at least that much higher as your knowledge and skills in your chosen profession improve as you continue your education until you are really polished.

Selling of course should always be a series of setting sales goals and achieving them on target. This I always do. Two specific examples of how and when I set sales goals and achieved them on target occurred in 1970 and 1971 when I was associated with the Earl Nightingale organization. I made up my mind that I wanted to make an impression on this particular organization and therefore intended to become their top distributor worldwide (They had over 4,000). I therefore set specific sales goals, weekly, monthly and yearly figures. Under the sales figure which was my goal for the month I would write on my "sales goal chart" my actual retail sales figures and then I would write whether I was in a plus or minus position for that month. For example let us say I set a goal for February to sell $10, 000 worth of product and I only sold $9,000.00 worth. I would write on my chart in **red** that I was minus $1,000.00 which I had failed to sell in February. This goal setting did in fact keep me on target and I did achieve my ultimate goal and was awarded two plaques naming me as top distributor for the years 1970 and 1971. So goal setting and the setting of specific sales goals is vital for success as a professional salesperson.

And now to our next Chapter 8 " Advertising and Public Relations."

8

ADVERTISING AND PUBLIC RELATIONS

"Sir, if they should cease to talk of me I must starve."

Dr. Samuel Johnson

"The advantage of doing one's praising for oneself is that one can lay it on so thick and exactly in the right places."

Samuel Butler

Of the above quotes I would say the second by Samuel Butler is the most applicable to the professional salesperson. Advertising and public relations are both extremely important tools to be used by the salesperson who aspires to become a truly great salesperson. Firstly let us all fully understand here and now that advertising oneself, one's ability, one's uniqueness, together with one's product or service is not being big-headed. In fact any person (and especially the professional salesperson) who believes that this is so has a big problem. They have a very low self-concept/self-esteem of themselves (now we will be dealing with this particular subject, self-concept/self-esteem in greater detail in Chapter 20). But for now you should fully understand that to tell the public about your accomplishments/qualifications/ abilities products and/or services either by paid for advertisements or press releases in the various local media where you are engaged in selling can greatly help you in your chosen profession and if you do not blow your own horn (as the saying goes) chances are nobody else will!!! Let us first deal with advertising. Many of the larger companies particularly in the automobile, real estate or insurance fields (to name just a few) have a regular annual advertising budget which draws attention to the companies' product or service and features different pictures of their sales staff in each advertisement. These advertisements are helping to sell the product or service together with the companies' sales personnel. These paid advertisements are indeed beneficial. Before leaving paid advertising let me give you and your companies two very special warnings. A lot of money can be wasted through advertising in the wrong media. In other words if you wish to advertise a particular product or service, first do some research. Find out what media **your particular** prospects for **your particular** product or service reads, looks at or listens to and only advertise in the appropriate media, which is going to help sell **your product or service** to **your prospects**. The next warning is to do with the wording of the advertisement. The general rule is "say what you have to in **as few words as possible**" and please take this advice from a thirty-year veteran professional salesman who has spent many years actually selling in the advertising industry. People just do not take notice or read or get the message contained in long worded advertisements. So be as brief, specific and to the point as possible with your advertisements, this way they will be more effective.

Now let us deal with public relations/press releases, etc. This is extremely effective too as long as it is professionally done. Here are a few examples of how you can acquire excellent public relations (which is all free and will also greatly help you to sell yourself and your product or service).

A. **Professionally prepared press releases** (preferably accompanied by a 10" x 8" glossy professionally taken photograph) for the local media. The local newspapers, magazines, radio and T.V. stations. For example let us presume that you have just qualified to go to your companies' annual convention by selling a certain dollar volume of your product or service. Write a professional article with a good heading (if you are not too good at writing, get some friend or maybe your sales manager to do it for you). For example the heading could read:

"Smith For Million Dollar Round Table Convention" and then the story (again just like the paid advertisement make this as brief as possible, precise and specific) and **always** accompany it with a photograph 10" x 8" glossy black and white. Provided these press releases are well done they will be printed and both you and your product or service will be brought to the attention of the public in general. You must realize that advertising and public relations is all a part of professional selling.

B. **Write a couple of short talks** and then contact your local Kiwanis, Lion's, Rotary Clubs or Chamber of Commerce and you will generally find they will be delighted to have you address them and usually the media will be there to give your talk adequate coverage.

C. On most local radio and T.V. stations there are regular **Talk Shows**. Contact these radio and T.V. station talk show hosts and offer to be a guest to speak on a particular subject (Obviously preferably related to your particular product or service). I have done many of these radio and T.V. talk shows and they do indeed help once again to promote you and your product or service.

D. Most professional salespeople use (what I would call **giveaways**) but which are really referred to as **premiums**. For examples key rings with a tag giving your name, address, product or service and phone number, diaries etc.

I have throughout my career consistently used advertising and public relations to help me in my selling. At least once a month I think up a good story, get a good photograph taken to illustrate the story, type a good my press release in a professional manner and take it together with an 8" x 10" glossy to all of the local media. If it is well written and properly-presented with a good photograph, I have always found the media willing to publish. Some stories which I have had in the press here in the Bahamas over the last ten years were I presented the prime minister with a set of books and this story with a picture got on the front page of our local morning newspaper. I have also done the same with the minister of education and culture here, the chief minister in the British Virgin Islands and the education minister in St. Kitts. I have also been featured in talk shows on radio and television in the Bahamas, Jamaica, Trinidad and Guyana. Advertising and public relations really does work so why not try it? Now!!! Today!!!

I do hope that you now fully realize the real importance of advertising and public relations for the professional salesperson. And now to our next Chapter 9 entitled "Referrals."

9

REFERRALS

"To-day I will multiply my value a hundred fold."

O.G. Mandino

"Never forget a customer: Never let a customer forget you."

Frank Bettger

"You can automate the production of cars but you cannot automate the production of customers."

Walter Reuter

Webster's Dictionary states that refer is "to direct to: to assign to: To have reference or relation to: To offer: As testimony in evidence; of character, qualification, etc. To allude (to)." And the American College Dictionary in part states that "refer" is "To Direct anyone for information, especially about one's character, abilities, etc."

I trust that from the above quotes and dictionary definitions you now understand what a referral or "Centre of Interest" (as I like to call them) is. However let us explain a bit further. I will endeavour to make this chapter as simple as possible as I have repeatedly said in other books the simplest things in life are really the greatest and apart from that this chapter about referrals is really simple. . . yet so important!! To put it in its simplest terms. When you have actually sold a prospect a product or service, he should (if you have done your job correctly and professionally) be delighted with you, your company and your product or service. So this is the best time to get from him a list of referrals (or names and addresses of persons in a similar position: Income bracket etc.) who would be interested in receiving further information about your product or service. He has bought and (believe you me) he or she will be only too delighted to give you the names and addresses of all of their friends, relatives, co-workers, and social friends **if you only ask for them**. If you have done a proper professional job as a salesperson and the close (which we will deal with in detail in the final chapter of this book, Chapter 27) has been a natural conclusion to your presentation, your new client will be delighted to give you many names of his friends, relatives , and co-workers for you to call on.

Doesn't this just make good sense? The main idea to get firmly implanted in your mind here as a professional career salesperson is that having completed your presentation and closed the sale, you should then ask for and· not leave without a list of names of your client's friends, relatives and co-workers whom they feel would like to purchase a similar product or service. Many companies who I have worked with offered a premium for each referral the client gave and who actually brought a similar product or service. When you leave your client armed with such a list of "referrals" it is going to make your job of prospecting so much easier. Can you just imagine calling (for example John Smith) and stating quite clearly and correctly that you were with (Fred Brown) yesterday and he recommended that you call him and set up an appointment to visit with him as he (Fred Brown) feels that the product or service which you have to offer could be of great assistance to him (John Smith). Isn't it obviously going to be much easier to get your appointment? Of course it is just try it and you will see what I am talking about in this chapter! So briefly just remember that before you leave a satisfied buyer or client (and if you are a truly professional salesperson each and every customer **should be fully satisfied**)!! Make a habit of getting a list of **at least** 6 names and addresses of his friends, relatives and co-workers. Get all the information about these future prospects that you possibly can, name, address, telephone number at home and work, type of work, number of children (if married), hobbies etc., in order that you will be fully prepared to speak to these prospects, these "referrals" and to sell them.

It is really common sense, isn't it? But you know what they say about common sense "the commonest thing about **common sense** is how **uncommon** it is!!"

When I was living in Toronto, Canada, I was working for a company called " All Canadian Home Products." This company sold just about everything for the home (as the name implies). However, they had no showroom, no warehouse and no advertising budget... all sales were accomplished by a direct marketing team. I was the top salesman in that team. My brief case contained just catalogues on **all** the products which I sold, order forms and finance company forms. The sales presentation explained that our company did not have the overhead expenses of the regular store which sold the same kind of products for the home. We had no showroom, no warehouse, and spent no money on advertising as the large stores did. However, we set aside a small sum of money for each product sold and mailed it to the customer who had given us the name and address of our new customer. When the sale had been completed and the finance paper work completed I then asked my customers for a list of names of their ends and acquaintances (social and from work and relatives). Explaining that for each one who bought from "All Canadian Home Products" they would receive a cheque for x amount of dollars. It was almost unbelievable how my customers compiled a list of prospects for me. Getting out old address books, Christmas card lists and looking in the telephone directory. I usually left with about 20/30 names, addresses and phone numbers of their friends and acquaintances. The next morn-ing in the office I mailed post-cards to these people whose names I had obtained from my customer the previous evening. The post-cards read like this: Dear Betty and Fred Smith, recently I had the pleasure of visiting with your friends Susan and Joe Brown and presenting a programme to them which they liked. They have given me your name as they feel that you too would be interested in such a programme. I will be calling you in a couple of days to set up an appointment. Yours sincerely, D. Paul Reilly.

I would mail all my post-cards and two days later call all of these people up and believe you me I always made appointments and out of these ap-pointments I got a large percentage of actual sales. So you see **"referrals"** are much more likely to buy than someone who you have not been introduced to.

So do follow the procedures as outlined in this chapter and keep on getting your **"referrals"** as it will help you greatly in prospecting and ultimately in selling a greater dollar volume of your particular product or service. Please do not forget your **"referrals"** and never leave a satisfied customer/ client without a list of at least **6 "referrals."** And now on the next Chapter 10 entitled **"Overselling."**

10

OVER-SELLING

"Today I will be master of my emotions."
O.G. Mandino

"You have not converted a man because
you have silence him."
John Morley

"I am not arguing with you, I am telling
you."
Anonymous

"If you wish to win a man's heart allow
him to confute you."
Benjamin Disraeli

Overselling is perhaps the worst sin of too many salespeople whom I have been associated with, especially during their training. It's an all too common error which must be corrected fully if one wishes to become a professional salesperson. Overselling can really turn a prospect off! So what is overselling? To put it in simplistic and blunt language it means "not knowing when to shut up!" Here's a cute story which will give you a laugh while helping you to understand the dangers of overselling. A young girl's family was upset because the young man that she was planning on marrying was an atheist and did not believe in God. The girl's mother on the other hand was very pious and religious "We'll not have you marrying an atheist" her mother said bluntly. "What can I do?" sobbed the girl, "I love him." "Well," said her mother, "if he loves you he'll do anything you ask, you should talk religion to him and **sell** him on the idea. If you keep at it long enough you can win him over." Several weeks went by, then one morning at breakfast the young girl appeared crying and absolutely broken-hearted. "What's the matter?" her mother asked "I thought that you were making such good progress in **selling** religion to your boyfriend," "That's the whole trouble" blurted out the young girl with tears streaming down her pretty cheeks "I **over sold** him. Last night he told me he was so convinced that he is going to study to be a priest."

I believe that this short story should help to illustrate the point that I'm making here. A properly prepared sales presentation by most companies will contain everything in it that if delivered correctly by a professional salesperson to a qualified prospect should automatically and quite naturally end in closing the sale. I have seen more sales people particularly when in training, when I'm taking them out on calls literally sell themselves into a sale where the prospect has said yes. (And it's at; this point that basically your sales presentation should stop and you should commence to write up the order). But so many of these people when training continue to sell trying to embellish the sales presentation, even going off at a complete tangent until they finally say too much! The prospect gets suspicious and backs out of the sale that he had agreed to earlier. I believe the main cause for this overselling is a lack of self-confidence (which we'll be dealing with in detail in chapter 20), and lack of confidence in or knowledge of the product or service as mentioned in chapter 1 ("preparation").

So finally remember to believe in yourself and your product or service, keep your cool and just as soon as you hear your prospect say yes (when you ask for the order) .... that is the end of your selling!! Just calmly get out your order pad and begin to fill in the details. The only time that you have to more selling (and sometimes start right at the beginning of your presentation again) is when you ask for the order and get a "no" or a "I'll think it over," but we'll be dealing with that in greater detail in our final chapter 27 ("Closing"). So for now just remember that as soon as you get that desired "yes" your selling ends, you make out the order, finalise the payment details, get the client's signature, pack up and with a pleasant phrase like "It's been a pleasure doing business with you and I look forward to calling on you when next I'm in our neighbourhood," leave.

Remember that the sole reason you're dealing with your prospect is to get that **sale**, you're not in there for a friendly chat, so do stick to your carefully prepared sales presentation and for God's sake don't oversell!! I do hope that you take particular note of this important point!!

In all honesty I must admit that I've never **oversold** a product or service as I've always been a **soft sell salesman** and never a **high pressure salesperson** I believe that I should state here and now quite adamantly that I don't believe in **high pressure methods**, in the long run they just don't work if you've done your job as a salesperson professionally the close should be automatic, you should never have to railroad anyone into a sale. However, all too often when I have been training salespeople and taking them out on calls, listening to them actually making sales presentations, as previously mentioned, I have seen over and over again sales people sell themselves into and right **out** of a sale! The prospect has actually said "yes, I would like to buy" and the sales trainee continues to sell instead of shutting up and getting out his order pad. The end result is usually a change of heart with the prospect and **no sale!** So please do not oversell.

11

RECORD KEEPING

"When found, take a note of."
Captain Cuttle — Charles Dickens

"All that time is lost which might be better
employed."
Rousseau

"I'd do so much you'd be surprised, if I
could just get organized."
Douglas Malloch

As we have already emphasized in Chapter 4 on "Planning" (which is very closely linked to this one of "Record Keeping") time is indeed money to the professional salesperson and time wasted is money down the drain. Proper and diligent "Record Keeping" is vital to all professional sales people to enable them to organize their planning. One of the first items that you should get is a prospect file to take your 3" x 5" prospect cards. Most good sales organizations will give these to their salespeople as they fully realize their importance. Every single prospect that you have should have a prospect card made out stating all of the relative information that you should have on this prospect, name, address, telephone numbers at home and business, married or single, approximate income and any other information that you'll need to help you sell your specific product or service. For example if you are selling automobiles you'll write down the type, model and year of his car. Also when he intends to change it. Write the date of your call and then file it in the appropriate section of your prospect file (say 5 months from now when the new model cars come out).

I cannot stress the importance of making out a prospect card on **all** of your prospects and of good record keeping for you cannot possibly remember all the details of your last call. When your prospect cards are filed correctly by the week or month, a great deal of your work is already pre-planned for you in your prospect file. Good record keeping, planning and organization are essential ingredients for the top professional salesperson. So if you haven't been doing this why not start today. It'll make your job that much easier.

I have always kept good records and I'm extremely methodical in everything I do. I always make out a 3" x 5" prospect card for every prospect and then write in abbreviate form the full details of each of my calls on this prospect. I then file them by the month. For example let's say a prospect asks me to call on them again in 6 months, I make a notation of this on the prospect card and file it in the appropriate month 6 months hence. I also keep records of important items in my diary, such as important appointments, speaking engagements etc. Another example of good record keeping has to do with my being the agent in the Bahamas for the excellent monthly magazine "Success Unlimited." This magazine is only available through yearly sub-scriptions which I take from clients. I have a small expandable file which has 12 pockets in it labeled January through December. As I sign up clients for annual subscriptions I file a copy of their order in the appropriate month. Thus I have next year's work (signing my clients up for renewal subscriptions for another year) all pre-planned on account of my methodical "Record Keeping." So "Record Keeping" is indeed important and now on to Chapter 12 "Service After Selling."

12

SERVICE AFTER SALES

"The Reputation of a man is like his shadow: it sometimes follows and sometimes proceeds him, It is sometimes longer and sometimes shorter than his natural size."
French Proverb

"What people say behind your back is your standing in the community."
Ed (E.W.) Howe

Your reputation as a professional salesperson is indeed important in your community, if you wish to reach the pinnacle of your career and stay there. Your reputation will depend to a great deal on what **after sales service** you give your **clients**. You notice I specifically said **client** here because my definition of a client is a customer who will continue to do business with you and repeatedly over many years order and re-order your company's products or services. This will only be attained by the salesperson who gives genuine service after sales. The day of the one shot deal with fast talking salespeople (in many cases conmen) who sold a product or service and never were ever to be seen by the customer again is over! Today more so than ever the buying public is more alive, alert and educated. Consumer protection associations and advocates (such as Ralph Nader) are constantly reminding the public to keep awake on their toes (so to speak) when buying products or services. So you my friend as a professional salesperson are going to have to be professional all the way and not just sell the product but give good after sales service too. It **will** pay off in the end and you'll get a great deal more business from your clients and their friends, co-workers, family, etc. They'll be delighted to refer them to you as mentioned in Chapter 9 "referrals." Remember getting the sale is really only the beginning of a long-lasting relationship with your clients **provided** and let's repeat **provided** you give that initial ingredient to all of your clients **after sales service** (even if it's only a friendly telephone call to see how they are, or if there is any other way in which you can be of service to them). Don't forget that great law for successful living, the law of "cause and effect" which simply states that our rewards in life will always match our **service**. This is indeed true especially for the successful professional salesperson.

When I was with the Nightingale organization selling audio/cassette personal development programmes I would always make it a habit to go back to each company with whom I had done business about 6 months after taking the orders from members of their staff and arrange to show them an Earl Nightingale film. I had the film on a handy compact super 8 mm projector so it was easy to actually carry it into the customers place of business and set it up. I found the customer appreciated this gesture very much indeed They felt that I still cared about my clients (as I was showing the film entirely free). The staff were also very appreciative and it helped to arouse interest again in motivation with these staff members who had in some oases stopped listening to the cassettes, and then in most cases I got a wonderful bonus without even asking for it or expecting it. Usually there would be some new staff members added since my original sales presentation and the company would invariably ask me to deliver a few more programmes. So you see I not only kept my clients happy by that extra **service** after the sale but it also led to more sales.

So never ever forget that **service** after the sale.

13

FURTHER EDUCATION

"The important thing is not to know more than all men, but to know more at each moment than any particular man. "

Goethe

"As knowledge increases, wonder deepens."

Charles Morgan

"If a man's education is finished he is finished."

E.A. Filene

I believe that the above quotes and in particular the last one by Filene sum up what I'm trying to tell each and every one of you. If you want to stay on top of your profession today you must keep on furthering your education of your company, its products and new sales methods. That's exactly why you are reading this book, right? Right! You should regularly attend all the seminars and training courses you can for people cannot stand still in this world, even if they want to. You're either going up or down! So which way do you want to go? The choice is yours! Nobody is smart enough to know everything (and that person who thinks he knows it all is a complete fool). We live in an ever-changing world and we must keep up with the times and keep on improving our knowledge and skill of our trade, our chosen profession.

Pablo Casals, the world's greatest cellist was asked by an interviewer not long before he died in Puerto Rico "why in spite of the fact that he was 96, the undisputed top cellist in the world, he still practiced daily." The simple answer from this great man was "I want to get better." And that's what it's all about. Improving our knowledge and skills, continuing our education and endeavouring to be a little better today than we were yesterday. Ever improving and traveling that winding staircase, upwards, upwards. You should make an effort to get every book you can on your chosen profession, get all the trade magazines, take courses and set aside time each day to read, to further your education for it will pay off well and its enjoyable too! Always remember that to stay on the top as a professional salesperson you must sacrifice something. You don't get anything in this world for nothing (the prisons of this world are full of those who believed that this is so). Success as a professional salesperson has a price to pay and you

must be prepared to pay that price in both time and money to further your education. Remember in the words of O.G. Mandino in Chapter 15 "The Greatest Salesman In The World," the scroll marked in Roman Numerals VII "Today I Will Multiply My Value a Hundredfold." Will you do just that today? Not for my sake but for your own sake, as it will help you to become more proficient at what you do for a living, one of the greatest careers in the world, that of a professional salesperson.

In motivation and sales training which are my specialties, I have been constantly furthering my education with courses, seminars, cassette programmes, books and magazines. I remember hearing Earl Nightingale saying in a recorded message that (and I quote) "Anyone can become an expert in their field in 5 years if they really want to." Well I took his advice and I have done exactly as he predicted, become an expert in my field of endeavour. When with the Nightingale Conant Corporation I attended several sales training and regional director seminars and distributor conventions in Chicago. I have learnt a great deal from many audio/cassette training programmes, a few of which are: lead the field, great ideas in selling, keep it simple salesmen, the master salesman, success for you, human engineering, the success system that never fails and many more. In fact I have a cassette library of over 200 tapes have a terrific library of great books such as the Living Bible, The Power of Positive Thinking, Psycho-cybernetics, I'm O.K. You're O.K., The Magic of Thinking Big, Etc., and I am always on the lookout for any courses, seminars, new cassette programmes or books which will assist me to acquire more knowledge and skills. I also subscribe to an excellent monthly magazine "Success Unlimited" which helps to keep me up to date in my profession.

I do hope you take this chapter very seriously as it is so important!

14

COMMUNICATION

"Speak little and well, if you wish to be considered as possessing merit."

French Saying

"The first ingredient in conversation is truth, the next, good sense, the third good humour, and the fourth, wit."

Sir William Temple

"He who sedulously attends, pointedly asks, calmly speaks, coolly answers and ceases when he has no more to say is in possession of some of the best requirements of man."

Lavater

Firstly I devoted a chapter (Chapter 7 on page 29) in my book "Success Is Simple" dealing in communication in general which I would firstly like to requote then I'll go into more detail as to how communication relates specifically to the professional salesperson. So here is in part sections of that chapter seven from "Success Is Simple."

"I believe that a lack of proper communication is one of the major causes of many of the problems in the world today. This is all too often evident in every type of person to person relationship, for example: husband/wife, employer/employee, parent/child, police/community, salesman/prospect, etc. " Now Webster's Dictionary defines to communicate as follows: "To impart information, to reveal, to convey" and the American Educator Encyclopedia states that communication is "the exchange of thoughts, feelings-opinions and information."

Communication requires a transmitter and a receiver. The transmitter transmits the thoughts, feelings, information and/or opinions and the receiver receives. Unfortunately so often in person-to-person communication the thoughts received are not the same as those transmitted. As a simple experiment get together with another person and speak to that person for five minutes. When you have finished ask the other person to tell you exactly what you have said or what thoughts you have transmitted. In most cases you'll be absolutely amazed to find out that most of what has been transmitted has not in fact been received. . . . the end result is a lack of communication!! So what is required in order to enable us to communicate more efficiently? After all as I continually say, communication is a vital part of your overall success programme. Well here are a few thoughts on how to improve personal communication with each other.

Firstly let us deal with the transmitter or the person who is transmitting the thoughts, feelings, opinions and/or information. The most important function of the transmitter is to be able to adequately express the thoughts etc. and therefore the following are essential:

(1) A good command of the English Language.
(2) A great deal of thought should be given to the thoughts etc. which you wish to express. Too many people speak without thinking. Think first, then speak.
(3) You must have a genuine desire to communicate… you must be sincere.
(4) You must understand body language… the silent language.

At this point I would like to discuss "The Silent Language" in detail as it is such an important part of good communication. Dr. Jurgen Rush, (a professor of psychiatry at the University of California) in his book "non-verbal communication" said in part "we communicate by means of some 700,000 non-verbal signs. Now when we consider the average vocabulary of most people we must surely realize why non-verbal communication plays such a vital role in the overall communication picture. Whether we fully realize it or not we telegraph (so to speak) our feelings and intentions to others." As I said earlier in this book when discussing "attitude" what's going on on the inside shows on the outside. We receive most of these non-verbal communications below the level of conscious thought, our subconscious computer-like minds evaluate them and serve them up as feelings. So much for non-verbal communication, And now to the final point of interest for the transmitter.

(5) You must use your voice by varying the tone to make a point, remember that the tone of your voice often conveys more accurately what is in your mind than do your actual words.

And now to the receiver:

(1) Again, just like the transmitter a good command of the English language is essential.
(2) The receiver must also have that genuine desire to receive, must be sincere and want to understand the thoughts, feelings etc. which are being transmitted.

(3) The receiver must learn to listen. As simple as this seems we don't listen enough today. We're far more interested in talking than in listening. But, do you know that the real art of good conversation is not speaking but in listening.

To impress this point on you I'd like to pass on some information that I heard on this subject by Dr. Ralph Nichols, Professor at The University of Minnesota, U.S.A. and perhaps the top authority in the world on human communication. Dr. Nichols states that on average some 2,000 reasonably complete and reasonably distinct messages are beamed toward each one of us in any given twenty-four-hour period. We pick up and relate to only twenty-five percent of these messages which are transmitted and aimed at us. So listening is important for effective communication.

(4) If when listening we hear something which we don't understand… we must query it… Don't pretend that you understand what has been expressed, what has been transmitted: If in fact you don't… don't be afraid to question! And finally in order for effective person to person communication to take place, it is essential for both the transmitter and the receiver to have a good empathy/ego

balance. Now what exactly is empathy/ego balance? Well let's first get some definitions. The American College Dictionary defines empathy as "mental entering into the feeling or spirit of a person: appreciative perception of understanding" and Webster's Dictionary defines ego as "the whole person; self; the personal identity." There was an excellent article written in the "Harvard Business Review" by David Mayer & Herbert Greenberg on this subject from which I would like to briefly quote:

"Empathy is the ability to imaginatively project ourselves into another person's situation. The persons who possess great empathy can sense the feelings and reactions of others and can change course (so to speak) as the situation changes. To have empathy one must be sensitive. Now ego means self. It should be understood at this point that we're not using the word ego as it is used in the sense of being egotistic. A person's ego is really the mental picture or self-image that one has of themselves and their abilities. It is the ego which gives you your drive toward achieving your goals. It is your ego which makes you need & want to achieve success; it's your propulsion. Now at this point you must fully realize and understand that both empathy and ego are highly important functions of the mind and are indeed powerful tools in any interpersonal situation. But the best communication will occur with people who possess a strong balance of empathy ego.

The key is balance!! Both a good ego drive and a deeply emphatic nature are vital for effective and successful communication. So how's your empathy I ego balance? If you find as many do a need for greater empathy is indicated, this is an attribute that can be developed with practice. In the novel, "To Kill A Mocking Bird" one of the characters said, "You never really understand a person until you consider things from their point of view, until you climb into their skin and walk about in it." Empathy does not require that you agree completely with all the ideas, feelings, and opinions of the other person. What it does require is that you appreciate them, respect them, understand them, and realize that you yourself might very well have come to similar conclusions had you been in their shoes. I'm sure that these few thoughts on the art of communication have been noted and that you will endeavour to apply them at all times for as I say repeatedly, effective communication is a vital ingredient in any success formula.

As William Shakespeare had Puck say in "A Midsummer Night's Dream," "I'll put a girdle round about the earth in forty minutes." Effective communication can help make the world your oyster, so concentrate and work on it as it will most definitely help you attain success."

Here's a couple of humorous stories on com-munication which I found amusing and in particular the latter two explaining what communication **is not!**

Joke No. 1 – "When you tell a man something it goes in one ear and out the other, when you tell a woman anything, it goes in both ears and out of her mouth."

Joke No. 2 – "Gentlemen" said the sales manager, "I've called you in to announce a big sales contest, it starts today and will run 6 weeks." The salesmen were excited and an eager person from the rear asked "What does the winner get?" "He gets," announced the sales manager, "to keep his job."

Joke No. 3 – "The persistent salesman finally managed to get into the manager's office. "I'm a very busy man," the manager said, "what's your proposition?" "I'm about to offer you something" said the salesman "that will make you a million dollars,"

"Well leave me your sales literature" said the manager, "Right now I am too busy to talk to you. I am working on a deal that should make me $200.00 in **real** money."

One of the best aids that a professional salesperson must have is a thorough knowledge of his prospects and their needs before he ever makes the call. He should have done his homework, he will then know what the prospect's actual needs are and exactly what he can afford, then through good **communication** he will be able to convince his prospect what product or service to purchase from him. By being a good communicator, a good listener, by understanding body (or the silent) language the professional sales. person will be able to find out and know exactly what the prospect really means which is not always what they actually say.

Two excellent examples from my own selling career should help you to understand more fully the importance of communication in professional selling and particularly in relation to actually closing a sale or sales. When I was selling encyclopedias, some of my very best prospects were school teachers. So I used to go to schools, approach the principal and set up an appointment after school to speak to all of the teachers. This is what we call a **group presentation** and it is a rather difficult selling situation as you have to be able to effectively sell to a group of maybe 10 to 15 people, all at one time. Good communication obviously played an important part in these group presentations to teachers for I invariably closed 90-100% of those to whom I spoke. This was an excellent closing average. The second example is drawn from my time selling audio cassette personal development programmes. I would first sell the idea to a company, usually getting them to agree to pay 50% of the cost of each programme provided the staff paid the other half. Once again this required a group presentation often to some 30 people and lasting maybe one hour. Excellent communication was again a very important part of these group presentations as once again I usually closed 80-100%.

So do please brush up on your communica-tion techniques as they can and will help you to make more sales, and now to Chapter 15 "Honesty."

15

HONESTY

"Here's the rule for bargains 'Do other men, for they would do you,' that's the true business precept."

Jonas Chuzzlewit
Charles Dickens

"I'm afraid we must make the world honest before we can honestly say to our children that honesty is the best policy."

George Bernard Shaw

"To be honest as this world goes, is to be one picked out of ten thousand."

Shakespeare

"Nothing will take the place of complete honesty, first, last and ALL THE TIME!"

Frank Bettger

I am going to start this chapter by suggesting that you first read Chapter 15 "Truth" in my book "Success Is Simple" and then come back to this chapter in this book as we'll now deal with honesty and truth as it effects the truly professional sales person and indeed the whole sales profession. This is a very important chapter and a very vital message.

As I have said repeatedly throughout the pages of this book I feel that to be a salesperson is indeed one of the greatest professions in the world. One of the noblest callings of mankind. However, we must face up to the problem that in our profession like any other it has throughout the years had more than its fair share of con-men and dishonest people, with no ethics or scruples whatsoever! Now this has got to stop once and for all in the selling profession. For your own sake, for my sake and for the sake of all salespeople throughout the entire world. I feel and we should all understand that we each and every one of us have an obligation to the profession as a whole worldwide to uphold at all times the highest moral standards. The day of the quick one time sale where all the facts are not revealed, (such as the great many land sale frauds recently) is over! You (as I do) should feel a grave responsibility to yourself and your company and the profession as a whole to be totally honest at all times.

Truly professional salespeople should stay with the prepared sales presentation, never adding in untruths or overselling (as mentioned in Chapter 10). Your first sale should only be the **beginning** of a long happy business association between the client (prospect) and the sales person with continuing **service after sales** (as discussed in Chapter 12). Never forget that one or two scandals in any profession be it in law, politics or selling casts immediate doubts on the profession as a whole. Just one or two dishonest salespeople in an area (usually just out for the fast buck) and not really professionals at all, can spoil it for every decent, honest salesperson in that area. So please, for your own sake, my sake and the sake of the whole profession worldwide, make a solemn resolution now, when selling, to always be honest with your client, to tell the truth, the whole truth and nothing but the truth, for in the end you will be a winner and a truly professional salesperson.

I am pleased to relate that I have all my life endeavoured to be honest and truthful in all of my dealings with my fellow men. However, one particular story comes to mind on how honesty really paid off when selling.

For several years I had been trying to get an appointment with the general manager of a large oil company to sell them some much needed motivational training courses for their staff. For years this particular manager would not even talk to me on the telephone, much less set up an appointment, however, being consistently persistent (Chapter 5) I kept calling every six months and finally it paid off for on one of these routine calls I found out that a new manager had been appointed. I obtained an interview with the new manager, without any problems and before I started to tell him about my courses I proceeded to acquaint him with the fact that I had been endeavouring to get an appointment with his predecessor for several years, but to no avail. When I had finished my sales presentation, he told me that he knew about my attempts to see his predecessor and that he appreciated my frankness, my openness and my **honesty**! To cut a long story short he became a very good customer, and personal friend so fellow salespeople in selling as in life **honesty** is indeed the best policy and now to Chapter 16 entitled "Be Innovative and Creative."

16

BE INNOVATIVE AND CREATIVE

"Originality consists in thinking for yourself and not in thinking like other people."

Sir J. Fitzjames-Stephen

"As soon as you can say what you think and not what some other person has thought for you, you are on the way to being a remarkable man."

Sir James Barrie

The contents of this chapter remind me of the story of a little boy and his mother who were in a store. The little boy wanted his mother to buy him a whistle "No," said the little boy's mother adamantly to the salesperson who was serving her. "I don't want a whistle for my little boy. The other day he nearly swallowed a friend's one," "Well," said the

"innovative salesman," "we have some nice bass fiddles I could show you.

A funny story but it perhaps illustrates my point to you. Now I hope that some of you don't get the wrong impression and feel that what I'm saying here is contradictory to what I told you about in Chapter 1 on "Preparation" that you must learn your prepared sales presentation word for word and stick to it. I'm not suggesting that you deviate from your sales presentation but you can add some extra selling tools by being innovative, creative and original as well as using your prepared sales presentation. That will make the difference between the mediocre and the great professional salesperson.

Let me give you an actual example of exactly what I mean. I have a great personal friend in Jamaica by the name of Tommy James. Now apart from being a beautiful and warm human being, Tommy is one of the top insurance salesmen (Life Underwriters) in Jamaica. Now here are two of Tommy's innovative creative and original ideas. Tommy used to be in the army so when a new batch of recruits are graduating from the Military Academy in Jamaica Tommy shows up on graduation day with his camera and he takes pictures free of all of the recruits, when he goes back with the prints to give to each of them he obviously broaches the subject of insurance and believe you me he sells a lot of insurance this way. Tommy also keeps in his diary all of his client's birthdays, anniversaries and other important occasions and on these days he always sends them a greeting card, here again with this simple innovative, creative and original idea, Tommy keeps in touch with his clients and when they wish to take out more insurance, whose name do you think comes to mind? ... That's right, Tommy James!

Yet another little example which I use myself is to read the newspapers very carefully each day and listen to the radio announcements and news programmes, when I read or hear that a certain person has received a promotion or has just arrived in town to take up a new position with a particular company, I write a brief letter of congratulations or of welcome. When I call these people a few weeks later I'm immediately recognized, I don't have to introduce myself and always have no difficulty in getting an appointment, and many times a sale. So do use that gold mine between your ears, your brain with its estimated 14 billion cells as it will help you to be innovative, creative and original and this will help you to get more sales. Here are a couple more of my own personal innovative ideas which were very successful in selling for me. I was once selling an audio cassette personal development programme especially designed and narrated by Dr. Maxwell Maltz, the program was designed specifically for children and was called appropriately "secrets." Now I used to go to the schools and sell the programme to the principal, then I would give him some specially printed forms to give to all the teachers to give to all the children to take home to their parents. Now the printed forms consisted of a message to parents, it sang the praises of the secrets programme which helped their children to obtain better grades and asked them (the parents) to fill out the details at the bottom of the form. Their name, address, telephone numbers etc. If they were interested in obtaining further information and to return it to school with their children. This idea proved to be very successful and I sold a tremendous volume of these programmes using this original method of prospecting and selling.

When I went into business for myself, selling encyclopedias, I obtained a rather nice bookcase to house the books which I sold in and I used to use it as I closed the sale as a special free bonus to all those who paid cash. This creative idea also worked well in obtaining a high volume of **cash sales**.

I suggest that you set aside some time each day when you can be **alone** for your thinking time. This will aid you to come up with your own innovative, creative and original ideas which will make you a winner and help make you a top professional salesperson and now to Chapter 17 entitled "Always A Professional."

17

ALWAYS A PROFESSIONAL

"Honour sinks where commerce long pre-
vails."

Oliver Goldsmith

"Never shrink from doing anything which
your business calls you to do the man who
is above his business, may one day find his
business above him."

Drew

Webster's Dictionary defines **Professional** as
"pertaining to a profession or calling, engaged in for
money as opposed to amateur" and the American
College Dictionary defines **professional** thus:

"1. Following an occupation as a means of
   livelihood or for gain.
2. One belonging to one of the learned or skilled
   professions."

However, the best definition that I have ever heard of a **professional** is "at your best regardless" and I have seen this definition in the form of a plaque on hundreds of sales managers desks throughout the world. Now what exactly does "at your best regardless" mean, well I believe it means the following:

That this world would be a better world to live in if every person no matter what their occupation were doing the absolute best of which they were capable, giving a baker's dozen (so to speak) each and every day. It really doesn't matter what you do for a living, being a delivery boy, an elevator operator or a bus boy in a hotel or for that matter the general manager of a bank, president of a large corporation, or a professional salesperson. The emphasis must at all times be on the word **professional**. You must always give of your best, do your job with all of the energy, enthusiasm, excitement, integrity, candor, dedication, honesty and professionalism that you can muster up. Never take short cuts, never lose your temper, always bear your goals in sight, always concentrate on your attitude. Compliment, communicate, solve the prospects problems, give excellent service, display the qualities of leadership, have sympathy, understanding and empathy and take the necessary action at the appropriate time to close the sale. Now this isn't always easy. There will be days when you don't feel

98

too good. You'll have to deal with uncooperative prospects and you'll have bad (sometimes very bad) days, when everything appears to be going wrong and all of your prospects are saying "no." It's on these precise types of days and with uncooperative and difficult prospects that you must make a very special effort, pull out all the stops and do your utmost to use every ounce of professionalism at your disposal, make a superb presentation and **get that difficult sale!**

Believe you me the extra effort will pay off, you'll have a client for life but even more important you'll have a tremendous feeling of inner satisfaction with having made that great effort in spite of how you felt and the attitude of your prospect and you will be able to comfort yourself in the fact that you handled the situation correctly, did not allow your emotions to rule you, rather you ruled your emotions, you did not allow yourself to adopt your customer's attitude, you kept your cool, your dignity, you disciplined yourself, were persistent, solved the problem at hand, got the sale, and proved that you are truly a great professional salesperson.

A specific example that immediately springs to mind relative to my being a true **professional** at a difficult time and how it paid off (as it **always** will) happened in 1972 in Jamaica. I was selling a motivational audio cassette training programme especially designed for life insurance agents. In the morning I had a group presentation to two offices of a particular insurance company in Kingston, Jamaica and at three o'clock in the afternoon of the same day I had another group presentation at the Mandeville office of the same insurance company. Now Mandeville is about 70 miles from Kingston. I had hired a car with air conditioning as it was during the summer months and extremely hot (temp. in the 90's and very humid) as it so happened the air conditioning was not working properly and so when I arrived at the insurance company office **slightly late** (because of repairs being done to part of the road), I was hot and extremely tired, the very last thing that I felt like doing was to stand in front of 30 insurance salespeople and speak to them for an hour. If I had had a choice I would have gone to the local hotel, had a refreshing shower and change of clothes, and a brief rest before going to the insurance company office for my group presentation. However, this was not possible, instead I combed my hair, wiped the perspiration from my face, straightened my tie, gritted my teeth, worked on my positive mental attitude and said to myself, " A real professional is at his best regardless!" To cut a long story short, I put everything I had into that particular presentation and when I was finished I got every single person to sign an order form (a hundred percent closing average). After the presentation I was sitting with the manager in his office and he told me that one of his agents had come to him after my presentation and stated that my talk had been the greatest that he had ever heard and that he was excited, inspired and motivated, when I heard that it really did give me tremendous inner satisfaction, for I knew that in spite of the very unideal situation that I had been in, I had done the very best of which I was capable. I had performed as a true **professional**! So professionalism in selling is vital to success and now to Chapter 18 "Patience and Tact."

18

PATIENCE AND TACT

"Forbear to mention what thou canst not praise."

Matthew Prior

"Never claim as a right what you can ask as a favour."

J. Churton Collins

"Tact consists in knowing how far we may go too far."

Jean Cocteau

"When I am tempted to criticize I will bite my tongue, when I am moved to praise I will shout from the roofs."

O.G. Mandino

Firstly, here's a little story to illustrate patience. After waiting for an hour, a waiter finally approached the customer and said, "what is it you wish sir," "Well sir" said the customer, "what I came in for was breakfast, but if dinner is ready now, I would like to order supper," and another short story to illustrate tact:

A lady at a cocktail party asked her new acquaintance to give her age, after he hesitated, she said, "come on, guess, you must have some idea." "I have several ideas he said, trouble is, I don't know whether to make you ten years younger on account of your looks, or ten years older on account of your intelligence." Boy did he have tact!

Now the American College Dictionary defines patience as "1. Calm and uncomplaining endurance as under pain, provocation etc. and 2. Calmness in waiting" and the same dictionary defines tact as "keen sense of what to say or do to avoid giving offence. Skill in dealing with difficult or delicate situations." So I am sure that from these quotations, humourous stories and dictionary definitions we can all readily see and fully understand that as professional salespeople we must always and at all times practice patience and tact in dealing with our prospects. We should make a determined effort to be calm and uncomplaining even when we are provoked as we will be on many occasions in our selling careers. We must be calm and serene when waiting, and let's face it selling requires a lot of waiting. As professional salespeople we have to be amateur psychologists, thereby feeling people out (so to speak) sensing their innermost feelings and then having a keen sense of what to do or say in any particular situation, in order to avoid giving offense or upsetting the prospect. This requires a skill in dealing with extremely difficult and delicate or sensitive situations which the salesperson will constantly have to deal with effectively if they are to turn a difficult prospect into a satisfied client. Patience and tact require the professional sales person to possess great empathy and control of their emotions. This is not at all easy, in fact in many situations it's almost impossible. However, these are two attributes which you must develop and practice daily if you wish to become tops in your chosen profession.

I repeat, it won't be easy, but it's essential to be a really great salesperson. So if this is an area where you need a little or (a lot of improvement, please go to work on it now as it will reward you with an abundance of love and respect and sales.

Without having to think at all, an example of how I really applied patience and tact in selling comes immediately to mind. Once again it happened on the island of Jamaica, when I was doing group presentations to insurance companies.

On this particular day I had two presentations in the morning in the Capital City of Kingston. (Having planned my activities well for that particular day). I had a taxi waiting for me after my second presentation to whisk me to the airport where I was to board a British Airways flight to Montego Bay some 120 miles from Kingston, where I had another presentation set up for 2:30 p.m. I got to Montego Bay, had a quick lunch at the airport and got a taxi to the Insurance Company office. I arrived at 2:00 p.m. (I always like to arrive early in order to relax, collect my thoughts and get my positive mental attitude working at optimum). I was in the manager's office talking to him, almost a half hour and then as 2:30 approached I suggested that we go into the agent's office to commence the presentation. At this point he calmly told me that he had forgotten to set up the meeting and that none of his agents were in fact at the office. Believe you me, I felt like exploding, but I didn't, I calmly looked in my diary and suggested that the meeting be set up again for the following Thursday, the manager agreed, I flew back to Kingston and the next Thursday flew back once again to Montego Bay, this time the meeting was set up as planned, the agents were very attentive and enthusiastic, the manager urged them **all** to buy one of my training programmes, and they all did. There was a total of 32 life insurance agents who each bought a programme at $215.00. Thus by being patient and tactful I had obtained a good order for a total of $6,880.00 and a tremendous feeling of achievement and inner satisfaction!

To add a final note by possessing these two fine attributes you will be a better person and you will find great things will start happening to you in every aspect of your life, business, personal and social. So my friend isn't it worth a try? You bet it is!

And now to Chapter 19, entitled "Showmanship."

19

SHOWMANSHIP

"Lend thy serious hearing to what I shall unfold."

Shakespeare

"One who is skilled at presenting things."
Webster's

What do you have to present? Your product and/or service, right? ..... Right! And you have your prepared sales presentation (Chapter 1) which you are ready to act out (Chapter 6) with proficiency and skill, now good showmanship can assist you greatly in delivering your sales presentation with the maximum impact and ultimately getting the sale. It's here where being creative and innovative (Chapter 16) really comes into its own. Good showmanship can and will make the difference between making a sales presentation boring or making it exciting, inspiring and convincing. So how can you be a better showman? Well basically by being a better actor by using your voice effectively to make a point, by varying your facial expressions, to emphasize a particular part in the sales presentation, by wearing a particular item of clothing or accessory, which really gets attention (such as a carnation in your buttonhole). By using your hands and body to gesticulate to again emphasize benefits of your product or service and helping you to present your product or service with skill. An excellent method which can be used effectively to assist you in becoming a superb showman is to have some samples with you to give a demonstration. Have a small super 8 mm projector with you to show a short film of your products and the background of your organization. Or display catalogues. Today many top organizations provide their salespeople with visual aids in the form of flip charts which can be used to emphasize what you are saying. To hold your prospects attention and assist you to be a good showman. But again you must be innovated and creative as previously stated. Let me give you an actual example:

My father (to whom this book is dedicated) at one stage of his career used to sell weighing scales for a large international organization. He used to enter the premises of his prospect, carrying a scale covered by a large black box. This large black box would be placed on the store counter and without taking the cover off and exposing the scale, my father would commence by talking in general terms to the prospect, gleaning from the prospect as much general information as possible which would be helpful in determining his needs, (after all selling is finding out What the prospect's needs are and filling those needs). All the time the prospect would be glancing at the box and wondering exactly what was underneath it. The cover would remain on for as long as possible and usually until the prospect couldn't bear the mystery any longer. Eventually the prospect would actually ask what was under the cover. Finally the cover would be removed to reveal beautiful gleaming modern new scales.

This was showmanship in action at its best, and of course showmanship is one of the most effective methods of 1. Getting the prospects attention (breaking the preoccupation barrier, chapter 1) 2. Keeping his attention throughout the presentation and 3. Closing the sale with confidence and professionalism.

An example of showmanship from my personal selling career is very difficult to pinpoint, as I believe I use it constantly every day, as it is such an important ingredient in all successful sales presentations. However, when I was with the Nightingale Organization, doing group presentations I used to first show Earl's award-winning film "The Strangest Secret." This really got the prospects' attention at the group presentation, and then after the film showing I would go into my presentation and ultimately close.

This film presentation certainly helped a great deal with my presentation and helped to inject some showmanship into the overall presentation.

So do be creative and innovative and learn and practice being a showman for it will greatly assist you in your selling career. And now to Chapter 20, "Self-Concept and Self-Esteem."

20

SELF-CONCEPT/ SELF-ESTEEM

"I AM nature's greatest miracle."
O.G. Mandino

"You are what you THINK you are."
Ben Sweetland

"We become what we THINK about."
Earl Nightingale

"Man is made or unmade by himself."
James Allen

"He that falls in love with himself will have no rivals."
Benjamin Franklin

The American College Dictionary defines self-esteem as "favourable opinion of oneself" and self-love as "the instinct by which man's actions are directed to the promotion of his own welfare."

I feel that it would be a good exercise for the readers of this book to first read Chapter 2 of my book "Success Is Simple" published by Cornerstone Library, Inc. of New York. We must all realize and fully understand that each one of us has a mental image or mental picture of ourselves; and in most cases our mental picture of ourselves is not at all good, it is not a healthy image. This is due in part to our environment, which is basically a very negative one and thus we constantly tend to under estimate ourselves and our abilities. Now we must substitute the positive for the negative. We must start to believe in ourselves and get a good healthy self-image of ourselves, by dwelling of ourselves, by dwelling on our past successes instead of past mistakes. We must understand respect and love ourselves (and by love I don't mean conceit but merely self-respect), before we can understand, love and respect others. So we can clearly see and understand that in order to be a top professional salesperson, it is vital to develop a good healthy positive self-concept, self-esteem or self-image. Two excellent books which I would strongly recommend you to get and study carefully on this subject are I. "Psycho-Cybernetics" by Dr. Maxwell Maltz, published by the Wiltshire Book Company of California and "The Greatest Miracle Book In The World" by O.G. Mandino, published by Frederick Fell, Publishers of New York.

If you read these two books and fully understand them, you will never ever again have a bad self-concept or inferiority complex and this is important to you in your chosen career. A brief quotation from "The Greatest Miracle in the World" should whet your appetite to get it and read it **now**! " A human being, my friend, is an amazing and complex and resilient organism capable of resuscitating itself from its own living death, many times, if it is given the opportunity and shown the way."

I would like to add that anyone who reads pages 103 to 107 from "The God Memorandum" in Chapter 9 of "The Greatest Miracle in the World" will shed all feelings of inadequacy forever!!

Now I would like to relate to you a short story about a salesman which appeared in Dr. Maltz's book "Psycho-Cybernetics" which fully illustrates exactly how having a bad self-concept places limits on progress and actually holds us back in our journey to the top. Dr. Maltz relates the story of a salesman, who for several years (working on salary and commission) earned $10,000.00 per year. He was a hard worker and a good and faithful employee, so the sales manager decided to put him in a superior territory with more people, more business and industry and better off financially, where it was assumed that he would get more orders and thus earn more commissions, receiving a larger overall pay check each month. As planned he was moved to this new territory but for five years he still earned how much? . . . . . Well exactly $10,000.00! Now this really mesmerized his employers and in particular his sales manager. So to complete their experiment they decided to now place the salesman in an inferior territory to the one in which he was originally. (Before they moved him to the better area). This territory had a smaller population, fewer businesses, less industry and was economically a poor region. As planned he was moved to the inferior territory and believe it or not he continued (regular as clockwork) to earn 10,000.00 per annum. Now this is a true story and it's told to illustrate that this particular person had a self-concept or mental image of himself as a **$10,000.00 a year salesman**, and until he changed his image of himself he could not progress any further.

I feel that the best example of how a good, healthy, positive self-concept is everyday helping me to sell new ideas to people (courses, lectures and seminars) can be seen by the fact that today companies who several years ago turned down my courses and seminars are today in fact agreeing to them. This I know is due to the fact that I have now got an excellent reputation. People now fully understand that I a) know what I'm talking and b) know how to effectively communicate my ideas and philosophies to my students. But I'm sure that the when selling, to always be honest with your client, to tell the truth, the whole truth and nothing but the truth, for in the end you will be a winner and a truly professional sales person.

21

PROBLEM SOLVING

"The only time I find people with no problems, is when I walk through a cemetery."

Dr. Norman Vincent Peale

"Discipline me in the habit of trying and trying again; yet show me the way to make use of the law of averages, favor me with alertness to recognise opportunity, yet endow me with patience which will concentrate my strength."

O.G. Mandino

" A matter proposed for solution."

Webster's

I would suggest that before reading this chapter you first read Chapter 9 on page 36 of my book "Success Is Simple." This will give you a general knowledge of problem solving and of my three-step formula: 1. Learn to react when there is no pressure. 2.

Learn to act aggressively to problems and 3. Learn to look at problems realistically.

Now let's look at problem solving specifically from the standpoint of a professional salesperson. Someone once said "no problem — no sale!" In other words, if there are no needs, no wants on the part of the prospect you can't solve the problem! So let's fully comprehend that solving problems or overcoming objections is vital if we wish to become tops in our chosen profession. Now objections can be divided into five basic types and they are: 1. Trivial or unimportant objections. 2. Hearsay objections (rumours) 3. Genuine objections 4. Prejudice (very difficult to handle as reasoning won't have any affect) and 5. Put off objections (postponing a decision). Let's see how to handle these five basic types of objections: 1. **Trivial Objections** — Here you must use what we call the "reverse method" by turning the prospects trivial excuse into an actual reason for buying.

2. **Hearsay Objections** — (Rumours). hen questions are asked by the prospect, answer them in great detail and refer them to one of your satisfied clients (who has already bought your product or service). This will quickly dispel rumours.

3. **Genuine Objections** — Let's face it, there will be genuine objections and the best method of dealing with them is to admit them, explain them and **sell the objection!**

4. **Prejudiced Objections** — We must face the fact, as professional salespeople, that people; have prejudices, and these types of objections care very difficult indeed to overcome as you can't reason with someone who holds a particular prejudice. However, you must deny it, if it's simply not true and be tactful in so doing.

5. **Put-Off Objections** — Making decisions is one of the greatest problems with prospects, so ask the prospect outright why he's not buying, if he hasn't stated why and then use the **Benjamin Franklyn Close**. The Benjamin Franklyn Close is a great selling tool and it works like this: Take a blank sheet of paper and draw a line down the middle, then list all of the reasons why your prospect **should not buy** in the left-hand column and all of the reasons why they **should buy** in the right-hand column. Work diligently on this exercise with the prospect and it stands to reason that since you have an excellent knowledge of your product or service (Chapter 1) you will know all of the wonderful advantages and you should be able to come up with far more reasons why the prospect **should buy** than they'll come up with for not buying. Thus you help the prospect to logically make the right decision. You overcome the objection, solve the problem and get the sale.

In general in dealing with objections please **cushion** your answers. Take it easy. Don't rush in too fast to knock down the prospects objections, you may hurt their ego and annoy them. If this happens you will not close the sale. You should take the objection and turn it into a question. A good rule to follow in solving problems in overcoming objections in selling is to analyze the objection and then get back to selling. The golden rule is "never get into arguments"!

When I resigned as chairman and chief executive officer of Goals International Ltd., I set up "The Human Resources Institute Ltd." I wrote my now famous six session "Road To Success" personal development programme and commenced conducting my courses. Gradually as more and more top executives attended my motivation courses and were excited and inspired, my reputation spread. However, in the meantime several other people had set up other training organizations and by all accounts were not doing too good a job. When visiting with companies (who has sent members of their staff to some of these other organizations for motivational training and had not obtained the desired results) I would often get a very negative attitude (and quite naturally) from the general manager regarding **all** motivational training. I would classify this as a "hearsay objection" (rumour) and immediately set about solving the problem, by giving my prospects several names of prominent executives who had already attended my course together with their telephone number. I would then request that they call these people in my presence. A couple of telephone conversations later the problem would be solved, and I would have several new students enrolled in my next course.

So never fear objections from prospects, welcome them for if they are handled effectively as outlined in this chapter they will become sales opportunities! And now to Chapter 22 "Self-Discipline."

22

SELF-DISCIPLINE

"Today I will be master of my emotions."
                                    O.G. Mandino

"He who reigns within himself, and rules passions, desires and fears is more than a king."
                                    Milton

"He that would govern others, first should be the master of himself."
                                    Philip Massinger

Nothing is more certain, more definite, more ultimate than the fact that if we really have a deep desire to become professional salespeople we must develop and practice on a daily basis the vital rule of "self-discipline." As I say in my book "Success Is Simple," we are all human beings and we are given free will at birth and, therefore, just naturally tend to do all the wrong things. However, if we wish to become successful as salespeople we must discipline ourselves in all of our actions. At the very beginning of our training, our preparation (Chapter 1.), we must discipline ourselves to learn our prepared sales presentation, to make up a good prospect list. We must learn everything we can about our company and its products or services. We must discipline ourselves to make calls. Yes, this is the one common denominator among all salespeople. They do not like to make calls. But we **all** know and fully comprehend that if we **consistently** make sales calls we will be successful and get sales. As professional sales people we have to discipline ourselves to do the things which the failures don't do. The very things that you and I don't like doing, but **which** we must do in order to keep on top.

Remember this, failures do not practice self-discipline, successful people must!

In dealing with our prospects, in being persistent, overcoming objections, we must discipline ourselves, always controlling our emotions rather than letting them control us, having patience and tact, sensitivity, empathy, humor, dedication and courage. We must discipline ourselves by putting aside time for planning, for innovative and creative thinking and for further education and finally we must take great care to discipline ourselves outside, of our actual working hours in order that we may be in top condition each day from an appearance, attitude and health point of view. This latter type of self-discipline is perhaps the hardest as salespeople have to (by the very nature of their profession) spend long periods of time away from home in strange territory where one has no friends. The all too easy way out is to go to a bar for company. This lack of self-discipline often ends up by the salesperson over indulging in alcohol and not being in good shape the next day for the task which lies ahead of him. I say this having had over 30-year experience as a professional salesman, I therefore, know and understand that the life of a salesperson can indeed be a lonely one. But I also know that seeking refuge in the bottle has ruined many thousands of good salespeople as it all too frequently becomes an addictive habit, a way of life (and often death). So my friends please take my advice, discipline yourself in every area of your life if you wish to become that which you have the God-given abilities and talents to become a top professional salesperson.

I (like any other human being who wishes to become successful) have had to (and continued daily to) discipline myself in order to achieve true accomplishment. A few specific examples of this taken from my selling career are the following:

Twenty years ago when in my early days of selling in England I didn't have a car, early on Monday mornings I would leave London by train for my destination. (Maybe Liverpool, Manchester, Carlisle, Devon or Edinburgh). My daily sales itinerary would be accomplished on foot. I used to walk an average of twelve miles per day, often in the most diabolical weather conditions, rain, snow, sleet, fog and cold biting north winds, but I disciplined myself. I kept at it and was successful. On really bad days (weather wise) I was indeed often tempted to go to the movies (as many salespeople are, and all too often do!). Once again, I would discipline myself and stay on the job selling! Selling! Selling! I always noticed that when I disciplined myself in this way I got a tremendous inner feeling of satisfaction that goes with knowing that you have done the right thing. Self-discipline has always, and will always help me to stay on top...... You see I savor success and don't welcome failure. Therefore, I fully understand both emotionally and intellectually that self-discipline is vital and now to Chapter 23 entitled "Some Very Vital Attributes."

23

SOME VERY
VITAL ATTRIBUTES

A. EMPATHY
B. COURAGE
C. HUMOUR
D. SENSITIVITY

EMPATHY "You never really understand a person until you consider things from their point of view."
Author of "To Kill A Mocking Bird"

COURAGE "I will persist, I will win"
O.G. Mandino

HUMOUR "I will laugh at the world."
O.G. Mandino

SENSITIVITY "The last best fruit which comes to perfection, even in the kind liest soul, is, tenderness toward the hard, forbearance toward the unforbearing, warmth of heart toward the cold, philanthropy towards the misanthropic Those who have no faith"

Richter

I am sure that the above quotes adequately illustrate exactly what these four vital attributes (which all people can develop and which the professional salesman **must** develop) are: A. Empathy B. Courage C. Humour and D. Sensitivity. And now let us deal with each of these attributes one by one:

Empathy — The American College Dictionary defines empathy as "The mental entering into the feeling or spirit of a person or thing. Appreciative perception or understanding." Do you make an honest effort to sense the feelings of your prospect? Are you appreciative and understanding of these feelings, even though you may not **agree** with them? You must understand that empathy does not require that you agree completely with the ideas, feelings or opinions of your prospect. What it does require is that you **appreciate** them, **respect** them, and **understand** them, so how is your empathy? Check it out for its a vital part of good selling.

Courage — Once again the American College Dictionary defines courage as "the quality of mind that enables one to encounter difficulties and danger with firmness or without fear, bravery." In Dr. Napoleon Hill's great classic "Think and Rich," he lists eleven qualities of leadership, and the very first is unwavering courage. So it is quite clear that if you wish to be leader in your profession, to be a consistently effective salesperson, you must have courage, do you have courage? Do you have guts? Are you willing to bet on yourself? Are you willing to risk failure in the interest of achievement? Or would you rather play it safe? Remember as Richter said "Courage consists not in blindly overlooking danger, but in seeing it and conquering it."

Humour — Again the American College Dictionary defines humour as "1. The quality of being funny. 2. The faculty of perceiving what is amusing or comical." If you wish to be and remain top in your field, as a professional salesperson, you must develop a keen sense of humour, you must be prepared to laugh with and at your prospects, laugh at yourself and at the world in general. O.G. Mandino in his best-selling book. "The Greatest Salesman In The World" says in chapter 14. "No living creature can laugh except man, trees may bleed when they are wounded and beasts in the field will cry in pain and hunger, yet only man has the gift of laughter, and it is his to use whenever he chooses." So do cultivate that habit of laughter.

Sensitivity — The American College Dictionary defines a sensitive person as "one who is readily affected by external agencies or influences and two having acute or mental or emotional sensibility."

In my opinion people in every walk of life today are all too insensitive to the problems and innermost feelings of others. If you wish to become an excellent professional salesperson you are going to have to be sensitive to the needs and wants of your prospects. You may like to ask yourself this question. Do I try to understand my prospects with all of their faults and failures or am I too quick to condemn without querying circumstances or trying to understand a situation?

Sensitivity is a most vital attribute for all professional salespeople.

Once again it is extremely difficult for me to pinpoint a particular incident in my selling career where I use these four vital attributes effectively in order to close a sale (or sales). However, after deep reflection I believe that one Sunday afternoon in Tortola in the British Virgin Islands I did use them and the result was truly magnificent. I was selling encyclopedias at the time and unfortunately I was rather ill, in fact my wife had to fly down from Nassau to take care of me, and nurse me back to good health. However, before getting ill, I had arranged to speak to the Parent Teachers' Association of the Tortola High School on a particular Sunday afternoon. On this Sunday I was feeling really ill. I had a temperature, I felt weak and heady, and yet I knew that I had a professional obligation to go to the P.T.A. meeting and speak to the parents who were taking the trouble to attend this pre-arranged meeting. Firstly, I obviously used courage in attending the meeting, feeling as I did. I opened my talk with a couple of jokes, using humour to relax my audience, and after I had completed my sales presentation, I held a question and answer period, where I handled all of the parents' and teachers' questions with all of the empathy and sensitivity that I could muster up. Everything went according to plan and as a result of that P.T.A. meeting I closed eleven sales for encyclopedias at $402.00 per set. So my afternoon's work had netted me a total $4,422.00 worth of business. Using those four vital attributes did pay off handsomely!

So there you have it four attributes which you **must** develop and put into practice on a daily basis in order to lead the field in your chosen profession. Empathy, courage, humour and sensitivity. And now to Chapter 24, entitled " Health of Mind and Body."

24

HEALTH OF MIND AND BODY

"'Tis the mind that makes the body rich."
Shakespeare

"The preservation of health is a DUTY. Few seem conscious that there is such a thing as physical morality."
Herbert Spencer

"He who has health has hope, and he who has hope has everything."
Arabian Proverb

Once again I wrote an excellent chapter, Chapter 16 in my book "Success Is Simple" on the subject of health, which I strongly recommend you read. As I said in that chapter a healthy mind and a healthy body go hand in hand, one without the other is no good. Now why is it of particular interest to the professional salesperson to have excellent health. To be in tip top physical shape, well I believe that selling is a difficult job and it requires a person to be physically fit in body and also have a good healthy positive mental attitude. Once again I would like to stress that it is difficult to have one without the other, so we must work on both by exercising them, that is both mind and body. To exercise the body, I have set out an excellent fifteen-minute daily exercise routine in Chapter 16 of "Success Is Simple" which I strongly recommend you follow on a daily basis. And to exercise the mind you must supply it with a constant flow of positive thoughts, set aside time each day for logical and rational thinking (daily thinking time) and endeavour to read a part of a good inspirational self-help book each day (daily reading time) for example "The Power of Positive Thinking," "The Magic of Thinking Big," "The Magic of Believing," "The Positive Principle Today," "The Greatest Miracle in the World" or "Success Is Simple." By being in top condition from a physical and mental point of view, you will feel great and will deliver your sales presentations with enthusiasm (Chapter 3) you will not tire during your hectic day. You will persist (Chapter 5). You will have and keep a better sense of humour (Chapter 23) and will as a result obtain more orders. So excellent health of both mind and body are indeed important factors to be considered for the professional sales person. To wind up this chapter let me tell you the story of the 80-

year old man who got a perfect score on his medical check-up. The doctor asked him how he kept in such good condition. "Well I was married 50 years ago," the man said, "My wife and I agreed that if I lost my temper she would remain quiet, and if she lost her temper, then I would take a walk. I attribute my good health to the well-known advantages of a daily hike in the woods."

You know today I am a better salesman than at any other time in my career and I sincerely believe (that apart from having so much experience and having matured with the passing of time) that this is due in great measure to my excellent state of health of both mind and body. You see today I don't drink any alcohol as I used to in rather large quantities. I don't smoke at all. Previously I used to smoke cigarettes almost nonstop. I also watch my diet carefully eating sufficient of the correct nutritious foods together with vitamin supplements and finally I exercise regularly **every day**. I can honestly say that I have never felt better in my whole life from a health standpoint of view. The net results are that I feel full of energy each day. I make more sales calls and my attitude is just terrific! I, therefore, get a lot more accomplished and also enjoy accomplishing it.

So much for good health and now to Chapter 25 entitled "Selling by asking questions."

25

SELLING BY ASKING QUESTIONS

"Each time he offered an objection or comment, I passed the ball right back to him with another question."

Frank Bettger

"By his method of questioning, Socrates changed the thinking of the world."

Frank Bettger

"You can do two things with a question"
1. Let the other person know what you think
2. You can at the same time pay them the compliment of asking their opinion."

Frank Bettger

As a famous educator once said "one of the biggest things you get out of a college education is a questioning attitude. A habit of demanding and weighing evidence... a scientific approach" and let's face it, selling is a science and must be dealt with as such. There is no doubt in my mind that one of the best methods of selling is by asking questions. This applies right at the very beginning of your call on the prospect before you actually commence delivering your prepared "Sales Presentation." If you will recall the very definition of selling as given in the introduction of this book is: A. Finding out what the prospect needs, filling that need and B. Educating. Well, what better method is there to find out exactly what the prospect's real needs are than by asking questions? As one great sales trainer I once knew said, "Don't sell by telling, sell by asking! " How right he was. When asking questions, the salesperson should always know in advance the **answers** they wish to receive from their prospects. Then knowing the answers that they're seeking the questions must be so structured so as to get the answers required. Always remember that when you ask a question, wait for an answer (EVEN IF IT TAKES FIVE MINUTES for the prospect to answer). Never ask another question until your prospect has answered the first one! When compiling your questions remember to ask open-ended questions which begin with the words, who, why, what, where, when and how. These types of questions will make your prospects think and answer your question.

Another very important area of any sales interview comes when you are trying to close and you are getting the old proverbial "put-off." Remember that at this stage the prospect does not usually mean what they say, for example "I'll think about it," so by asking open-ended questions you get answers and the real meaning of what's inside the prospect's mind. Selling by asking questions is, therefore, indeed an important sales tool, which you should use with true professionalism. This method will help you to avoid arguments, to avoid talking too much and it will aid you in finding out exactly what's in the prospect's mind. What are his needs and wants. Finally by asking questions and letting the prospect answer it shows that you respect the prospect's point of view. This will make them feel important and thus you will receive in return the prospect's admiration, respect and business.

Once again I have always sold by asking questions at the beginning of the interview with the prospect in order to ascertain their needs and wants. Specific examples of some of these questions when selling motivational courses and seminars are as follows: Do you have an attitude problem with your employees? Are they goal-oriented? How would you say their self-esteem is? Are your employees accomplishing as much each day as they should... Are they planning their activities? How effectively are your employees able to communicate? Do they fully understand that great law which lies at the foundation of all achievement "the law of cause and effect"? Are your employees efficient at solving day to day problems? Etc. Etc. I am sure you get the picture! By asking these questions I get a composite of my prospects needs and wants but you will also notice that the questions are meticulously chosen as I know the answers in advance, which I require in order to sell my particular service. You see I know that my courses and seminars help to improve employee attitude, assist them in setting specific short and long-range goals. My courses cover in great depth, planning, organization and systems, person to person communication, the law of cause and effect, problem solving etc. so do put together your **own** prepared list of questions as it will assist you greatly, in determining the prospects needs and wants.

Please note and use this excellent selling technique and now to Chapter 26 entitled "Action."

26

ACTION

"I will act now."

                    O.G. Mandino

"The Shortest Answer Is Doing"

                    Lord Herbert

"The end of man is an action and not a thought, though it were the noblest."

                    Carlyle

"Strong reasons make strong actions."

                    Shakespeare

"Do it now!"

                    W. Clement Stone

There's another old saying that "nothing happens until somebody **does** something" and I want to impress upon you in this second last chapter that nothing good is going to happen to you as a professional salesperson until you **do** something positive. . . until you take

action. . . until you go out and **make sales calls**. . . until you put the contents of this book into **practice** on a daily basis! You know there are millions in this world who are fully aware of exactly what they must do in order to achieve success and yet they never seem to make the grade! There are also thousands of sales people who possess all the necessary knowledge and skills and yet they never become great salespeople. The simple yet tragic reason for their failure is that they don't realize the tremendous importance of **action**. You see it's not just enough to **know** the right things in this life, you must **do** the right things to succeed at any undertaking. Another old saying says "talk is cheap and money buys the whiskey." So having read the chapters of this book and learnt how to be a successful salesperson you must now commence putting these principles and rules of good sales-manship into **practice** on a daily basis! You must concentrate on your preparation and planning. Take great care of your personal appearance and be enthusiastic when you act out your prepared sales presentation. Set daily, weekly, monthly and yearly sales goals and be persistent in achieving them on target. Pay attention to advertising and public relations. Don't forget to obtain "referrals" after you have closed each sale and then keep your "records" in order. Service after sales and furthering your education in your chosen profession should always be foremost in your mind. Practise daily honesty, self-discipline, patience, tact, empathy and courage. Be sensitive and also humorous in your daily dealings with your clients. Remember always and at all times to be a true professional, solve your prospects problems, ask questions, help them to make the right decisions, and use showmanship. Practise the very important art of communication, keep your body and mind healthy, be innovative and creative and finally **close that sale**! You will effectively do all of the above provided you **make those calls**, and take **action** on a daily basis, for "actions speak louder than words!"

An excellent example of how I used action in my long selling career occurred when (for personal reasons) I resigned as chairman and chief executive officer of Goals International Limited, immediately upon -my resignation I incorporated "The Human Resources Institute Limited." I then commenced writing my now famous "Road To Success," personal development programme, next I had some quality brochures printed and before I had finished writing the course I commenced actual sales calls on companies, and started to enroll students for my first course. The result of this instant **action** was that by the time I had completed writing my course I had a full complement of students ready to take it. I conducted the course, it was an outstanding success. And now several years later it's (without a doubt) the best course of its kind available. So you see **action** did pay off! And now to our final chapter, Chapter 27 entitled "Closing."

27

CLOSING

"Assume a close, having a winning attitude."

Frank Bettger

"If my approach is right, if I have been able to create sufficient INTEREST and DESIRE, then when the time comes for ACTION the prospect is ready and eager to buy."

Frank Bettger

This, the final chapter, my fellow salespeople is indeed the most important... getting the final commitment, closing the sale, for if there's **no close**, there's **no sale**, and if you can't close a sale then al l of the other basic rules of good salesmanship as outlined in this book will be useless. A good self-concept (Chapter 20) confidence in oneself and the way in which you have conducted the entire sales presentation will help you immensely to **ask for the sale!** Yes, indeed don't be afraid to **ask** for the sale, it's one of the most effective ways of closing. Here are a couple of tips on closing.

By giving a series of choices at the end of your presentation (such as "Would you like the blue or the red?" "Will we deliver to your home or office?" "Will that be cash, cheque or charge?")

You will be helping your prospect to make a decision and thus helping the close. If your prospect appears to be having difficulty in finally making a decision, you might like to use "The Benjamin Franklyn Close" (As mentioned in Chapter 21 "Problem Solving" in dealing with put-off objections). It's a very useful closing and selling tool. You must remember that in closing **no sale is a sale without finalizing the payment procedures**. You must either get cash or cheque in full payment or credit card details or a deposit with the order, together with full details, specifically set out regarding balance of payment... 30 days, 60 days, etc. Otherwise you will not have closed the sale. You will have a promise instead of an order! So please remember **"No sale is a sale without the cash"** as Life Underwriters always say "Check with APP" meaning payment with the application. Finally please realize that the close should not have to be be-laboured or pushed. Instead it should be the natural logical and rational conclusion of an effective sales presentation. **Never use pressure**, I implore you!! If you can't close, the ultimate answer is that you have not completely sold your prospect. You should, therefore, go back to square one and start **selling** again. If, however, after a couple of attempts to close you still aren't successful, pack up and with a cheerful farewell move on to your next call, remember your time is money, not every prospect will buy, and there's no sense in knocking your head against a brick wall with some prospects when there are others waiting nearby.

Now obviously being a successful salesman for so long, it stands to reason that I am an excellent closer and I believe that this is due to the fact that I do a good job throughout the entire sales presentation and, therefore, the close is automatic. However, here are a couple of actual closing methods which I have used successfully. When I was with the Earl Nightingale Organization, I used to sell a particular sales training audio — cassette programme for Life Underwriters (I have referred to this previously). Now this programme actually contained a written guarantee from the Nightingale-Conant Corporation, stating that if the insurance agent used it in accordance with the written instructions and did not increase their production by a minimum of 50% the company would refund their money and take the programme back. (That's how effective the programme was. Now I would do a lot of group presentations with this programme and my close went like this, I would simply say "hands up all of you who would like to increase your production by 50%?"

Well I'm sure that you can see the picture, obviously everybody would put up their hands and I would simply hand out the order forms. An example of a typical **multiple choice close** occurs when selling subscriptions to "Success Unlimited" magazine. At the end of the short extremely effective presentation, there are the following **three choice closes**: 1. Would you like book A. or book B. as your free gift? (Note a free book is given to each subscriber who signs up for one year's subscription to the magazine). 2. Will we deliver the magazine to your home or office? 3. Will that be cash, cheque, or credit card? I do hope that you fully understand the grave importance of closing a sale for (I repeat once again) if **there is no close there is no sale!!!**

So my good friends I sincerely hope and pray that you have all learnt a great deal from reading this book and that you will continuously put what you have learnt into practice and go on to become a professional salesperson that every member of this great profession can be proud of!

In closing I would like to pass on to my fellow salespeople throughout the world an Irish poem which I feel will adequately convey my feelings to all salespeople wherever you may be. It is entitled **"An Irish Blessing"** and it goes like this:

"May the road rise to meet you
May the wind be always at your back,
May the sun shine warm upon your face
And the rain fall soft upon your fields,
And until we meet again may God hold you,
In the palm of His hands!"

DPaulReilly.com
for more Books, Time to Think & Winners Club information.

Welcome to
THE REILLY INSTITUTE
Home of "THE WINNERS CLUB" & "THE TIME TO THINK CLUB"

By joining either The Winners Club or The Time to Think Club, yous can acces a wealth of dynanmic lectures, interviews, and daily motivational programs featuring Dr. D. Paul Reily on your computer, ipad or mobile device.

**** YOU CAN ACCESS THESE AND OTHER MATERIALS BY JOINING THE WINNERS CLUB ****

Dr. D. Paul Reilly

D. PAUL REILLY Ph.D., Msc.D., D.Sc.F.

Dr. Reilly, who was born in Dublin, Ireland, is a specialist in the field of Human Resources Development and Behavior Modification. He is an Author, Broadcaster, Columnist, and Training Consultant. He has authored several books including Success is Simple, The Science of Selling, and Time to Think, Volume I. He is also the Author, Narrator and Producer of "Time to Think" a daily program for radio. His TV series Broaden Your Horizons has aired on PBS in the USA and several networks worldwide.

Over the years, Dr. Reilly has been associated with many world leaders in the field of Human Resources Development, Motivation, & Personal Development, and has worked with such internationally recognized experts as Earl Nightingale and Dr. Maxwell Maltz.

Dr. Reilly is an articulate, creative, intelligent, sensitive, and sincere writer and lecturer, who is dedicated to motivating people to develop their full potential ... reach their goals ... find their individual success. He is a truly inspirational author, broadcaster, columnist, and educator, with a highly distinctive and unique style, which people can relate to.

Dr. D. Paul Reilly

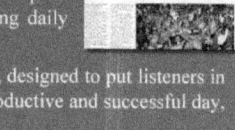

Popular Educator, Philosopher and International Motivational Expert, Dr. D. Paul Reilly, has been a long time favorite in The Bahamas, as well as world wide, with his powerfully positive, inspirational, motivational and thought-provoking daily radio programs and newspaper columns.

Now Dr. D. Paul Reilly's radio messages, designed to put listeners in the right frame of mind to have a most productive and successful day, are available for your benefit directly.